CW01082998

Women in Music

The Singer-Songwriting Divas:
the stories of the reigning
queens of music in an industry
of underrepresentation

Florence Sydney

© Copyright 2021 - All rights reserved.

The content contained within this book may not be reproduced, duplicated or transmitted without direct written permission from the author or the publisher.

Under no circumstances will any blame or legal responsibility be held against the publisher, or author, for any damages, reparation, or monetary loss due to the information contained within this book, either directly or indirectly.

Legal Notice:
This book is copyright protected. It is only for personal use. You cannot amend, distribute, sell, use, quote or paraphrase any part, or the content within this book, without the consent of the author or publisher.

Disclaimer Notice:
Please note the information contained within this document is for educational and entertainment purposes only. All effort has been executed to present accurate, up to date, reliable, complete information. No warranties of any kind are declared or implied. Readers acknowledge that the author is not engaged in the rendering of legal, financial, medical or professional advice. The content within this book has been derived from various sources. Please consult a licensed professional before attempting any techniques outlined in this book.

By reading this document, the reader agrees that under no circumstances is the author responsible for any losses, direct or indirect, that are incurred as a result of the use of the information contained within this document, including, but not limited to, errors, omissions, or inaccuracies.

For Grace & Ben

Table of Content

Introduction

When you turn on the radio or think of what artists are topping the charts, you might think a lot of female artists are dominating the scene. Dua Lipa, Cardi B, Billie Eilish, Olivia Rodrigo are some of the current 'it' artists of the moment. However, regardless of what we see, statistically, the industry is still male dominated, even in 2021. The truth is that women in the 1970s, 1980s, 1990s and 2000s and even today have to put in twice as much effort to get half as far as men. It's constantly thinking of new ventures, new genres and new looks to keep relevance in the music industry that makes the stories of the superstars of yesterday, relatable to the superstars of today.

What makes such powerhouse singers, such as modern artists like Amy Winehouse and Beyonce, hold the same legendary status as their predecessors like Cher and Madonna is their ability to not listen to the status quo. To break the mould set by an industry that pigeonholes women. Another similarity with all these women is the level of heartbreak discussed in their music, the age-old topic of being wronged by a man. While we all deal with broken hearts in very different ways, these ladies know how to transform their emotions into incredibly captivating songwriting, making you wonder why you could never put words together in the same manner they have.

Take, for example, Stevie Nicks. The reasons behind her breakup with Lindsey Buckingham are arguably no different than why every other couple on the planet ends up breaking up. But the way she describes her heartbreak in songs "I Don't Wanna Know" and "Silver Springs" put into words the intense emotions women feel after the end of a loving relationship. Nicks lets her listeners know they're not alone in their feelings, and this plays a reason for why she's a superstar in her own right.

Furthermore, there's Beyonce, with her 2016 album, Lemonade, informing the world she was cheated on by her husband and constant collaborator, Jay-Z. Her lyrics shocked fans with this revelation that someone like Beyonce would ever be cheated on, along with how a seemingly loving and happy relationship could be tainted with an affair. The lyrics for the album deep-dive into her betrayal, her anger, and her broken heart. She sang and wrote about infidelity that made women who have been in similar circumstances know their feelings, emotions, and reactions are valid.

The art these ladies create stays with us; it's why they're familiar to people across generations. It's when you put on "I Feel the Earth Move" by Carole King to boost your energy when you're getting ready. Or "Brass in Pocket" by The Pretenders when you walk down the street, knowing that you look like an 11 out of 10.

The women I chose to include in this book are the powerhouses that are the creators of our go-to songs, the ones who have songs for every mood and event you attend, and influence and inspire many other female artists to create their own art.

Their unique and bold personalities make them iconic. The wonder in the way they put words together on a page, then to say those words with unparalleled instrumentation.

Moreover, it's not just their music careers where the women showcase their skills. They are multi-faceted, with a majority of the singers venturing into other businesses, displaying their talents and personality in other areas, and trying to make changes in the world.

It's why I wrote this book and why you're here now.

However, while reading the stories of these artists, it's crucial to shed light on the music industry's dark side, as it's not just the biographies of these talented women but also the trials and tribulations they've faced as women to stand out in the crowd of a male-dominated industry.

A Brief History of Women in the Music Industry

On the outside, it may look like things are positive for women in the music area of the entertainment business. While there are some achievements, it's essential to look back and remember what came before and how we got to where we are now.

So many factors have gone into oppressing women in the industry. For example, they were being valued for their attractiveness over their skills, believing they were not creative enough or intelligent enough to know the technicalities of the industry. It would be nice to believe women no longer experience these inherently sexist beliefs. While progress has been made, there definitely is not enough.

During the mid-1800s, there was blatant sexism and misogyny against women wanting to create music. The belief was that a woman's biology was reason enough for her to be incapable of composition. However, near the end of the century, women were able to teach music to children. The growth in women songwriters emerged during the late century. However, their names for their work were ambiguous, as women still dealt with difficulties being taken seriously as songwriters.

Fast forward to the early 1960s, women were seen as performers of music; however, the creative process of becoming a songwriter, playing an instrument, or being a producer was seen as a faux pas and acceptable exclusively for men. This resulted in men forcing lovey-dovey pop music to the masses, telling female audiences how to live their lives, and being the gatekeepers of their emotions. More specifically, being in love and belonging to a man. The songs "My Guy" by Mary Wells and "You Can't Hurry Love" by The Supremes are classic examples of this narrative.

However, by the late 60s, a trailblazing set of female singer-songwriters emerged, wanting to break free from the male-dominated restraints of pop music to create music on their terms and writing their own songs based on personal experiences such as Carole King and Joni Mitchell. Such female artists like Joni and Janis Ian struggled with prejudice by trying to break the mould female musicians were placed in. They wanted to be seen as artists who created amazing pieces of music without their gender interfering.

The 1970s carried the momentum from the late 60s, and in the 1980s, more improvements came in the form of Madonna. Known as the "Queen of Pop," Madonna changed the pop music landscape with being her authentic self, the opening of sex and sexuality, and the concept of reinventing oneself for a new album cycle.

All-female bands grew in popularity in the 70s and 80s, more so in the rock genre with the likes of The Runaways, Heart, and The Go-Gos. The growth of all-female bands or just a woman playing an instrument in a band of men was met with resistance. These ladies were not taken as serious professionals and didn't receive as much coverage as all-male bands did. For example, the opening guitar riff on Heart's "Barracuda" is iconic. But not many people believed guitarist Nancy Wilson could be talented enough to play that opening riff. This was still the same story during the beginning of the 1990s, especially in the grunge scene.

Looking back at the grunge era, most bands that would come to mind are all male, and maybe a mention of one female band. Bands such as Hole, L7, and Babes in Toyland made the grunge genre their own, delving into topics of feminism and sexism. Grunge women were seen as risqué due to their loud sound, vocals, and personality. Moreover, they demanded your attention and took up space in the rooms they were in. Their music played a crucial role in the Riot Grrl culture, a punk feminist group whose prominent 'leader' was Kathleen Hanna of Bikini Kill.

As grunge died, bubble gum pop moved back into the mainstream, and girl groups were all the rage. The Spice Girls and their "girl power" movement, along with Destiny's Child's songs of female empowerment, made changes in the music industry and how women worldwide valued themselves.

Today, it may seem that women are dominating the music charts more than ever, but unfortunately, that's not the case. A study conducted in 2020 by the USC Annenberg Inclusion Initiative found that of the top 600 songs on the Billboard's year-end Hot 100 chart for each of those six years, only 22.4 % of the 1,239 performing artists were women.

Additionally, even in recent years, talks of sexism and discrimination are still present. In 2015 during a Billboard Women in Music event, superstar Lady

Gaga called the music industry a "boy's club." Musician Bjork has mentioned the work of women in the music industry goes unnoticed. She even detailed that the work she creates is credited to the men she works with. Usually, because she only sings in live performances, the public doesn't consider her a producer or someone who plays any instruments.

Post Me Too and Times Up, the public and media have re-evaluated the treatment of women in the music industry, including Britney Spears, Janet Jackson, and Taylor Swift. At the same time, it may seem that women talking about their experiences with sexism and misogyny, while trying to grow and maintain their music careers is making a difference. It's the actions that need to be taken to fully see the results of women being on an equal playing field with their male equivalents.

Facts and Figures

Before we dive into the biographies of the nine divas in this book, it's essential to acknowledge some of the current issues within the state of the music industry. Moreover, it's vital to mention some of the women behind the scenes in music who deserve appreciation.

Women as Producers

As of 2021, women in producing and songwriting are on the decline compared to previous years, with diversity and representation being stagnant, even when it arguably appears to be otherwise.

There are plenty of male producers that are household names, including Max Martin, Quincy Jones, Nile Rodgers, and Timbaland. Whereas their female counterparts are rarely known, or there is a shock when it's revealed one of your favourite songs or albums has a woman as its producer.

Therefore, a small list of female producers that are long overdue to receive recognition for their musical contributions is as follows.

Sylvia Robinson: Known as "The Mother of Hip-Hop," Robinson not only was a successful R&B artist with her hits including "Pillow Talk," she's also known as the producer to Sugar Hill Gang's "Rapper's Delight" and Grand Master Flash and the Furious Five's "The Message," bringing the sounds of the urban areas of New York and New Jersey to the mainstream.

Linda Perry: While she may be considered the most recognizable female producer, Perry is most likely best known for being the lead singer of the band 4 Non-Blonds. However, she's had a very successful career producing albums and songs for other artists, including P!nk, Adele, and Britney Spears.

Tokimonsta: Also known as Jennifer Lee, she's well established in the Los Angeles dance and electronic music scene as a DJ and producer. She's also the first Korean American producer to receive a Grammy nomination for Best Dance/Electronic Album for her record Lune Rouge. It's also quite common for Tokimonsta to remix popular songs of famous artists, including Beck's "Wow" and Duran Duran's "Last Night in the City."

Sylvia Massey: Massey is one of the very few female producers in the rock and metal genres. She's worked with world-renowned artists, including Tom Petty, Prince, and the Red Hot Chili Peppers. She currently works out of her own studio as an independent producer and engineer. Massey is also an educator, teaching others her skills in production, mixing, and engineering to inspire others to pursue their passions in the world of recording.

It's pretty apparent that the problem is the lack of these female producers receiving proper recognition or being in demand for their work compared to male producers. The quality of their work is there, but moving forward, there need to be more spaces for women to hone and develop their skills in a music studio.

Women in Songwriting

A lot of female singers nowadays write their own songs, whether it is by themselves or with others. When these artists do collaborate with other songwriters, however, how many are female?

The answer is not many. For example, on Beyonce's critically acclaimed album, Lemonade, one of her most popular songs on the album, "Hold Up," has 15 songwriting credits. Only two of those songwriters are women (one being Beyonce herself).

It's well established that singers these days double as songwriters, but what about those women whose career is defined by just writing songs for others? Once again, look no further than below.

Kara DioGuardi: DioGuardi is a prominent songwriter behind many mainstream early 2000s pop-rock songs, with over 320 songs released in her catalogue. She has written songs for Hilary Duff, Celine Dion, and Christina Aguilera. DioGuardi is also recognized as a judge for a brief stint on American Idol.

Diane Warren: Known as a significant contributor in music creation, Diane Warren has won numerous Grammys, Emmys, Billboard Music Awards, and Golden Globes. She's also inducted into the Songwriters Hall of Fame. Some of her biggest, award-winning hits include "Rhythm of the Night" by DeBarge, "If I Could Turn Back Time" by Cher, and "I Don't Want to Miss a Thing" by Aerosmith.

Cynthia Weil: Known for being a co-writer with her husband Barry Mann, Weil has been in this collaborative partnership with her husband for over 60 years. All the songs she has co-written are epic love songs. With legendary songs such as "Here You Come Again" by Dolly Parton, "We Gotta Get out of This Place" by The Animals, and their most successful song, "You've Lost That Lovin' Feeling" by The Righteous Brothers.

Bobbie Gentry: Gentry is a retired country artist credited for being the first woman to write and produce her entire discography. Her claim to fame is her Southern Gothic Country song, "Ode to Billie Joe." She retired from music and public life in the early 1980s, but the way her legacy paved the way for women to have creative direction in their art lives on.

Black Women in Music

It would be a disservice not to dedicate a section of this introduction to the recognition of Black female songwriters. It is well documented that the foundations of the music genres we know today are credited to Black people, with their songs and instrumentation appropriated by white artists' to much greater success.

Unfortunately, the gross amount of racism and sexism Black female artists receive has hardly changed. Arguably, the racism and sexism Black women receive are on a level of their own.

Current main stays are Doja Cat, Megan Thee Stallion, and Cardi B. While there are endless amounts of Black men rising on the charts. From Drake, Kanye West, Lil Nas X, and The Weeknd. The way the public perceives these artists' music differs as well. While no one bats an eye at The Weeknd singing about his heavy partying lifestyle and all the women he beds, Cardi B. and Megan Thee Stallion releasing a song about women being sexually liberated and explicitly saying what they want in the bedroom blows up in the pop culture circuit with some praise and a lot of criticism.

Even more so, it's male and female critics alike who place Black female artists under a microscope with heavier scrutiny compared to men of any race and white women. For example, during her time in The Supremes, Diana Ross was hit with critiques that she 'wasn't black enough.' Whitney Houston was booed during the Soul Train Awards because she didn't reach the 'standards' of what a Black female pop singer should be. Even today, the success of Lizzo's music is overshadowed by comments about her weight. Essentially, all the critics throughout the years have been telling these women how dare they try to be successful and not fit these imaginary standards of Black women.

Furthermore, if we look at the statistics with Black women behind the scenes in music production, the numbers are not so great. A 2020 study conducted by the USC Annenberg Inclusion Initiative found that across 70 major and independent music companies, just 13.9% of top executives were from underrepresented racial/ethnic groups, 4.2% were Black, and 13.9% were women. Additionally, as of writing this book, only three Black women have been inducted into the Songwriters Hall of Fame (Sylvia Moy, Valerie Simpson, and Missy Elliott).

So, what do all these statistics and stories mean? What's the point of adding them to this book about the lives of the super famous and successful singers?

Well, the information above gives you an understanding of the times women were living in and how these women have adapted in an ever-changing industry to maintain relevance. It's still very much a patriarchal world all these women are living in. There has been some growth over the years, but the barriers divas like Cher had to break are still similar to the ones Bjork had to break as well.

On A High Note

This book is curated with a handful of incredibly talented and legendary female singer/songwriters who have inspired and entertained generations of women and men.

My goal with this book is to educate and entertain you in the rise to fame of these incredible singers and question how the lives of these divas impact how the music industry treats women in this day and age. Are women being treated as equals? Is there an increase of women pursuing careers in all fields of the music industry? Is there more diversity? What do the stories of these iconic artists tell us about where music has been and where music is going?

Without further ado, let's get into the lives of the divas that have shaped and redefined the music industry. So, sit back, read, and enjoy. And maybe have some of their music playing in the background.

Florence Sydney

Chapter 1: Amy Winehouse

It's 2007, and the 50th Grammy Awards is taking place at the Staples Centre in Los Angeles, California. It's a who's-who event of A-listers across all genres and careers in the music industry. Kanye West, Natalie Cole, the Foo Fighters, and Cyndi Lauper are all in attendance.

A big contender this night is Amy Winehouse, who isn't there. At least, not physically. At the time, Winehouse had just left a treatment centre for drug addiction, resulting in difficulties for her to obtain a work visa to travel to the United States for the awards show. When she's finally approved for a visa, the timing is too little, too late, so Grammy executives put the backup plan of her performing via satellite in London into motion.

At 3:00 am, London time, Amy takes the stage, performing her hits "You Know I'm No Good" and "Rehab." Amy was becoming notorious for being unfit to sing during live performances by slurring her words and staggering around the stage. When she walked to the microphone in her mini black dress and black high heels, all those concerns fell to the floor. Her vocals are top-notch, adding her own flair as she shimmed her shoulders and swung her hips to the jazz band accompanying her.

Throughout the night, Amy was sweeping the board, winning the awards for Best Pop Vocal Album for Back to Black, Best Female Pop Vocal Performance for "Rehab," Best New Artist, and Song of the Year for "Rehab."

1

So far, Amy has won four out of her six nominations. During her final nomination, Record of the Year, camera shots of Amy caught her looking unbothered and not thinking she'd win. While in Los Angeles, Tony Bennett announces the winner. Amy Winehouse. The cameras cut to Amy, and she paces while looking at the floor before stopping right at the microphone and looking up at the screen. Her bandmates erupt in cheers and utter happiness behind her, running and hugging each other. Amy's jaw drops, and her eyes fill with tears. She's absolutely shocked. Amy turns around and embraces one of her bandmates, and others join along with her father. As her mother runs on stage and hugs her, the crowds start chanting her name. Amy, stunned, grabs the microphone and thanks her parents, her husband, record label, producers, and the City of London, all to the soundtrack of a cheering audience.

Amy makes history that night, becoming the first British woman to win five Grammys and the fifth woman to join the exclusive list of most Grammys won by a woman in one night. Back to Black rises up the charts, with more people falling in love with Amy's voice, provocative personality, and modern lyrics combined with 60s inspired instrumentation. She is a new powerhouse vocalist and songwriter who has changed the landscape of the music industry for a brief moment in time.

During the time of writing this book, 2021 marks the 10th anniversary of Amy Winehouse's death. She was an artist who brought jazz back into the mainstream, along with a distinctive voice who left us far too soon.

Amy, Amy, Amy

Amy Jade Winehouse was born on September 14, 1983, to parents Mitch and Janis Winehouse in Enfield, London, England. Along with her older brother, Alex, she attended Osidge Primary School and was brought up in the Jewish faith. The Winehouse's were devout Jews, enrolling Amy in Jewish Sunday School. However, Amy's confidence in stating what did and didn't work for her appeared at her young age, telling her family she didn't believe the extra education made her any closer to learning more about her Jewish faith. Although, she could often be seen wearing a Star of David necklace during live performances in later years.

Growing up, Amy was surrounded by music, and she developed her love of jazz music from the jazz musicians on her mom's side of the family. Mitch and Janis encouraged her interest, and many nights Amy and her father would sing her favourite song, "Fly Me to the Moon," by Frank Sinatra. Mitch began singing the song to her at around two years old, and anytime Amy needed to cheer herself up, she sang herself Frank's classic hit. Amy also listened to icons Etta James and Billie Holiday, and while her love of jazz and soul knew no bounds, she became drawn to R&B and hip-hop artists such as TLC and Salt-N-Pepa. Inspired by the girl groups, Amy and her best friend Juliette formed their own group called Sweet 'n' Sour. Obviously enough, Amy was Sour, and Juliette was Sweet; the two girls practiced singing their R&B hits although they never made any plans to perform in front of people, and as quickly as their group formed, they disbanded.

With her love of music growing, 12-year-old Amy made the decision to apply to the performing arts school, the Sylvia Young Theatre School, in secret. Eventually, she received notice that she was invited to audition. Upon telling her family, no one was upset that Amy went behind their back, they were excited. Amy's grandmother suggested she sing "Oh the Sunny Side of the Street" by Louis Armstrong. With no professional training in singing, Amy's parents helped her practice for her audition. Different breathing techniques ensured she hit all the notes. After her successful audition, Amy became a student.

While attending the Sylvia Young Theatre School, her independent, devil-may-care attitude got her into trouble. The headmistress told her repeatedly to take out her nose ring and earrings. While talented, Amy never applied herself and was always daydreaming. Soon, it became clear that the theatre school was not for her, and she left to attend The Mill Hill International and then the music school, BRIT. Once again, the school wasn't in the cards for Amy. She began a battle with depression and cutting the insides of her arms, along with discovering marijuana. Because of these factors, she left school before she could graduate.

While her personality and schooling didn't match, Amy's friends could rely on her loyalty and always being there to lend a hand. However, she could have moments of being arrogant and frustrating. Amy also gave her no-limits approach to anything she did in her life. In her late teens, she developed bulimia. Amy became friends with a group of girls whose pastime included gorging on rich, savoury foods and immediately making themselves sick afterward. While most of the girls eventually found ways to end their eating disorders, Amy never did.

During this time, Amy started playing around with her brother's guitar when he was out of the house.

She bought one for herself and began writing songs. After dropping out of school, Amy jumped around from job to job, becoming an entertainment journalist at World Entertainment News Network and playing in a jazz band with frequent gigs at the Cobden Club.

At one of her gigs, music manager Nick Shymansky attended. Captivated by her voice and talent, he met her after her show and offered to help her record some demos to secure a record deal. Amy, caught off guard, questioned the legitimacy of Nick's offer. But knowing music was her passion and not wanting to miss an opportunity, Amy went along with it anyway. After recording her demos, her boyfriend at the time, singer Tyler James, sent her demos off to an A&R representative.

19 Management, spearheaded by Simon Fuller, heard Amy's demos. Impressed with Amy's talent, he wanted to sign her immediately. Which he did, and Amy Winehouse, the professional singer, was born.

What is it About Men?

When Amy began working at 19 Management, Simon kept her work under wraps for her to grow and develop her craft. That was until Island Records A&R representative Darcus Breese accidentally heard her voice on a record. Darcus fell in love with her voice and knew he wanted to sign her to a record deal. But since Amy's identity was a secret, Darcus spent months trying to track down the person to the voice he heard. After six months, he finally did.

Once Darcus tracked Amy down, he signed her to Island Records. Not long after, Amy and her production team began working on her first album, Frank. During the creation of her first album, Amy worked alongside Darcus and her producer from 19 Management, Salaam Remi. While her work relationships with her producers helped Amy form the direction of her debut album, she kept her stubbornness and unwillingness to differ on her vision of Frank. Named after one of her favourite artists, Frank Sinatra, Amy wrote all the songs on the album, minus two covers. With lyrics about love and romance, with a dash of humour, Amy sang with a vampy, sultry voice, with the album's atmosphere sounding like it came straight from an underground speakeasy.

Frank was released on October 20, 2003, exclusively in the United Kingdom, selling over 250,000 copies and eventually going platinum. The lead single, "Stronger Than Me," is about Amy calling out her man who isn't reaching her standards. Followed by "Take the Box," "In My Bed/You Sent Me Flying," and "Pumps/Help Yourself," which all performed well on the charts.

Amy's promotional work on the album included performances at Glastonbury Festival-Jazzworld and the Montreal International Jazz Festival. She received two Brit Award nominations for British Female Solo Artist and British Solo Act before winning the Ivor Novello award for "Stronger Than Me" as Best Contemporary Song. Moreso, Frank became shortlisted for the Mercury Music prize in 2004.

While the album was a critical and commercial success, Amy wasn't happy with the marketing and the way executives at Island Records would override her creative decisions.

Even as more people became familiar with the name Amy Winehouse, the UK began to learn about Amy's unfiltered personality. For an album filled with a soulful voice, Amy's everyday voice was raunchy and brash. She told interviewers that people would have to get used to her and spoke about her father's infidelities that led up to her parent's divorce years earlier, and inspired songs on her album.

However, her bold personality didn't hinder any future accomplishments. Frank was released in 2004 to European countries and Canada, then in Australia and the United States in 2007.

Back to Black

With the success of her first album out of the way, Amy was ready for round two. However, her new lifestyle choices started to get in the way. While promoting Frank, Amy began hitting the party scene. She was constantly spotted going to bars and pubs, leading to her beginning to show up to performances and promotional events drunk and performing inebriated, not performing at all, or simply not showing up.

Living her new party lifestyle, Amy began to frequent her favourite spots across Camden. On one such night at her usual place where she'd play pool and surround herself by the sound of 60s music playing from the jukebox, Amy met Blake Fielder-Civil, a train wreck crashing right into Amy's heart.

From Frank to Blake

Amy and Blake's relationship was a whirlwind and volatile romance from the start. Since meeting that fateful night at a Camden pub, Amy and Blake were inseparable, despite Blake already being in a relationship. The intensity of their affair caused Blake to end his relationship with his girlfriend. Blake, a music video assistant, loved the party lifestyle just as much as Amy did. He also had a love of hard drugs and introduced heroin and cocaine to Amy. As Amy had a self-described addictive personality, it didn't take long for her to become a frequent user of the drugs and develop an unhealthy dependence on Blake.

With Blake, her partying life escalated. During the making of Frank, Amy did drink but mainly was focused on smoking marijuana, which she credited as inspiring the jazz sound of the album. However, since one of the few drugs of choice Blake didn't use was marijuana, Amy gradually stopped smoking and drank more as a replacement. Coincidentally, one small piece of goodness came out of their party ways. The bars they usually went to played a lot of 60s girl groups and Motown, causing Amy to fall back in love with the music of that period. Plus, the excessive drinking inspired the blues and R&B lovesick sounds of her second album.

In the studio, getting ready to create her new album, Amy was introduced to Mark Ronson, a music producer whom executives at Island hoped Amy would get along with. The pair hit it off, creating the perfect 60s blues and R&B sound Amy wanted. During this time, Blake ended his relationship with Amy to rekindle his relationship with the girlfriend he left her for. Amy, already deep into the drinking and drugs introduced by Blake, spiralled further, even leading to significant weight loss.

Amy's management team became concerned with her wellbeing and encouraged her to go to rehab for her drinking. Amy refused and seemed to get her drinking under control by herself. As she came to terms with the end of her relationship with Blake, she poured her soul into the work of her second album. Completing the album in just five months, Back to Black was inspired by what was taking place in her life during that time. Songs like "Back to Black" were inspired by her breakup with Blake, while her management's attempt to have her enter rehab inspired her to write the first single off the album, "Rehab."

Back to Black was released on October 27, 2006, and exploded onto the charts, topping number one in the UK and reaching top ten positions around the world. Selling over 16 million copies worldwide, the album was a huge commercial and critical success. It was bringing Amy mainstream recognition and praise for her songwriting capabilities in telling her story about the toxic relationships and substance abuse issues she faced with such rawness and authenticity. Not to mention mixing the retro sounds of the 50s and 60s soul and R&B that sounds fresh and modern.

Along with the success of her album, Amy developed her signature style. A massive 60s inspired beehive weave attached to the top of her head as her hip-length black hair flowed, coupled with her bold and exaggerated pitch-black winged eyeliner. During a time when every pop star has blonde hair and crop tops, Amy's look is eye-catching and even inspiration for high fashion.

As her stardom grew, Amy was nonchalant with her fame. She couldn't care less about the media coverage or the paparazzi. She just wanted to sing. But as her personal demons flourished, she became a cog in the pop culture machine that was more dedicated to watching her fall than helping her up.

Love is a Losing Game

As Amy hit superstardom, every part of her personal life became documented and analysed. During her time apart from Blake, Amy began a brief relationship with chef/ musician Alex Clare. Once their relationship ended, he told his side of their relationship to a tabloid magazine, News of the World, going into graphic detail about their relationship and criticizing her for breaking up with him.

The reason for the breakup? Amy rekindled her romance with Blake, and on May 18, 2007, the couple got married in Miami Beach, Florida. However, the honeymoon period didn't last long; Amy revealed in interviews that if she was drunk and upset enough, she'd get into physical fights with Blake. Her constant battle with addiction and her wild actions on stage and in public became a media and paparazzi gold mine. Physical evidence is proven when paparazzi photos are taken of them bloodied and bruised out on the streets of London after a fight, even though Amy claimed hers were self-inflicted.

While her personal life is filled with controversy, the promotion and recognition of Back to Black had no limits. Her record-breaking Grammy wins, Best Female Artist at the Brit Awards, and two more nominations for the Ivor Novello Awards, and the Mercury Prize showcased her incredible talent and artistry. But it became overshadowed as her drinking and drug use hit a new low with her grandmother's death and Blake getting arrested and convicted of grievous bodily harm, which resulted in him spending eight months in jail.

Prior to Blake's incarceration, the couple went on a bender, with Amy being hospitalized from an overdose of heroin, cocaine, ecstasy, alcohol, and ketamine. Her overdose led her to an admission to rehab with no results.

After being released from rehab, her live performances became out of control and unpredictable. Due to missing Blake, Amy either performed as she did before her drug problems worsened, or she was painful to watch. At the National Indoor Arena in Birmingham on November

15, 2007, appearing half an hour late with a drink in hand, Amy stumbled through her show, continuously asking for someone to top up her glass. She was dropping her microphone and crying when dedicating her song "Wake Up Alone" to her husband. Her words became more slurred throughout the night, and the crowd started booing her as many of her fans exited the arena, leaving Amy crying and throwing her microphone.

Unfortunately, this wasn't her only performance when she was unfit to play. Numerous shows followed similar antics to the point where she cancelled the remainder of her tours on the grounds that she needed to rest and take care of herself.

New Man, New Ventures

In January of 2009, Amy was no longer using drugs, coming to the realization that her entire marriage to Blake depended on their use. While on vacation in the Caribbean, the paparazzi took photos of Amy on vacation with another man, proclaiming she'd found somebody else to love. Meanwhile, Blake, still in jail, caught word of the news and proceeded to file for divorce on the grounds of adultery, with their divorce becoming finalized on August 28, 2009.

Once Blake was no longer in her life, things for Amy seemed to get a tiny bit better. She was no longer using drugs, but drinking was still a significant factor in her life. While she continued to enter and exit rehab for drinking, with the help of her parents and management, she cycled through periods of sobriety before drinking again.

Throughout 2009 and 2010, she made numerous appearances on stage, TV, and concerts. Amy also began a relationship with writer and director Reg Traviss, a romance that was finally healthy. During the year, Amy promised the public a new album in January of 2011.

While the album didn't happen, Amy pursued different business opportunities. She created Lioness Records, a record label after being inspired by the singing of her goddaughter, who she also signed as her first artist.

Tears Dry on Their Own

In late 2010, Amy began a comeback tour in Europe, but after repeated drunken performances, Amy cancelled her European tour and returned to her Camden home.

On the morning of July 23, 2011, Amy's live-in bodyguard went to her room to check up on her. She appeared to be sleeping, so he left her be. Hours passed, and at 3:00 pm, he checked on her again and found her in the same position from hours ago. As he got closer, he realized Amy did not have a pulse and was not breathing. He proceeded to call an ambulance. When paramedics arrived, they pronounced her dead at the scene.

Further investigations concluded that Amy's death was a result of alcohol poisoning. Due to a drinking binge, the coroner detailed Amy's body contained 416 mg of alcohol per decilitre in her blood—more than five times the legal driving limit.

News of Amy's death sent shockwaves around the world, with an outpouring of grief for an incredible artist gone way too soon. Despite the constant criticism in the media over her addictions, many of those around her hoped she would eventually get better. Coverage of her death also mentioned that since she died at age 27, she had now joined the infamous 27 Club, a group of famous musicians including Kurt Cobain, Janis Joplin, Jim Morrison, and

Jimi Hendrix, who all died at age 27 due to drugs and alcohol abuse.

Following her death, her family established the Amy Winehouse Foundation, a charity organization whose mission is to educate and prevent youth from abusing drugs and alcohol, along with helping those in recovery.

In 2015, a documentary about her life, entitled Amy, was released. The film was quite successful and won an Academy Award for Best Documentary Feature.

Over the years, Amy's influence can be seen in the waves of unconventional female singers becoming known in North America and worldwide, including Adele and Florence and the Machine. Furthermore, she paved the way for female singers to be more assertive about their opinions, creativity, and perspectives on what they want to create in the recording studio.

Her legacy lives on in the way she made retro music her own but also mainstream during a time when over-commercialization and synthesizer beats were all the rage in pop music. It's also her unapologetic personality, her loudness, and her wit that made her relatable to women everywhere. She's the voice for women to stand up for themselves and be authentic without caring what anyone else thinks of them, and while she may be gone, the impact she left on the world isn't forgotten.

Chapter 2: Carole King

It's a cold day on December 6, 2015, in Washington, D.C. Yet, inside the Kennedy Centre Opera House, there is nothing but warmth. The opera house is filled to the brim with people for the yearly Kennedy Centre Honors. The purpose of the event is to honour those who have contributed significantly to the performing arts that result in affecting American culture as a whole.

One of the honourees that year is Carole King. She's the last honouree of the night, with performances and speeches from those she's impacted throughout her life. While Carole appreciated the loving praise she's received, organizers saved the best for last. Aretha Franklin, known as the 'Queen of Soul,' walked on stage to a piano. Carole, who didn't know Aretha would be in attendance, was shocked, and her jaw dropped. As Aretha began to play the notes of a very familiar song, Carole covered her mouth and put a hand over her heart.

The song in question is "(You Make Me Feel Like) A Natural Woman," one of Carole's hit songs she wrote specifically for Aretha back in 1967. Carole was feeling all of the emotions as she listened to Aretha sing, she had tears in her eyes, and she sang and swayed back and forth to Aretha's voice. Standing in her balcony seat, Carole encouraged Aretha to belt those high notes, moving her body so dramatically one might think she could fall.

By the time Aretha has finished singing, she received a standing ovation from the audience. While she blows everyone away, it's the moment between Carole and Aretha that's special. Her performance shows the mutual respect both icons have for each other and the song. "(You Make Me Feel Like) A Natural Woman" is one of Aretha's greatest hits and one of Carole's landmark songwriting achievements.

The song is one of many Carole has written for others to perform, but this moment, in particular, stands out because it showed the impact of her songwriting capabilities and the way in which she not only proved to the world that women could write hit songs and iconic albums about womanly experiences. Carole also had no problem offering her talents to other women so they could achieve their own level of superstardom.

It Could Have Been Anyone

Carol Joan Klein was born on February 9, 1942, in Manhattan, New York City, to parents Eugenia and Sidney Klein. Carole's upbringing saw her living modestly; during the Great Depression, her father left his job as a radio announcer for better job security and became a firefighter, while her mother was a housewife. Struggling to get by but too proud for handouts, the Klein's lived by the means that they could afford, with a young Carole helping her mum at a moment's notice.

In her childhood, Carole's mum decided to teach piano lessons to earn some extra money and even taught Carole how to play, as her constant curiosity about music continued to grow. As Eugenia taught her, at just four years old, Carole was already a piano wiz. Even though her parents couldn't afford proper lessons, they discovered Carole had absolute pitch, a rare skill of being able to recognize a musical note by memory. Impressed with her ability, Sidney boasted

15

about it at social events, even asking Carole to demonstrate her talent to friends.

The talent for music was clearly in Carole's blood. At four years old, she began writing her own songs and playing them on the piano. Moreover, her exceptional talents extended to more than just music. When Carole started school, she was more academically advanced than her peers, and she was bumped from kindergarten to grade two.

A Moment in the Spotlight

In 1950, Carole was eight years old and got her first act as a performer. Her mum brought her to audition for The Horn and Hardet Children's Hour with friend Loretta Stone. The two girls sang, "If I Knew You Were Comin' I'd've Baked a Cake." Loretta sang harmony, and Carole sang melody and played the ukulele. The producers chose them to perform on the show, with the reaction from the crowd leaving Carole with joy. Still, Carole found that she felt more comfortable on stage with Loretta than if she was by herself, and she disliked being the centre of attention. The performance also prompted Carole to create her first stage name, Carol Kane, as her birth name didn't give her the wow factor she was looking for.

Carole moved from performing arts schools to regular public schools before settling at James Madison High School. Regardless of her decision to attend public school, she was still obsessed with music. Carole was constantly listening to the radio for inspiration, which played a role in why she decided to volunteer for her high school talent show. Composing songs for others and performing herself, the satisfaction she received from the performances gave her the drive to push herself further in anything she could accomplish musically, which is how she got the idea to start a band.

The band, called the Cosines, consisted of herself along with classmates Iris Lipnick, Lenny Pullman, and Joel Zwick. After school, the band practiced their vocals and choreography at Carole's house, with her composing and arranging their songs. Although dedicated to the music they were creating, the band was locally known and only performed at school events. During her time with the Cosines, Carole realized that she still preferred creating rather than performing her songs. Soon, Carole felt that enough was enough, and feeling more triumphant in her skills than ever before, she decided it was time to break into the music industry.

Some Kind of Wonderful

Determined to be signed, at 14, Carole would travel to New York City from Brooklyn, going to any and every record company and showing them her songs in the hopes that someone would be interested. Her dream came true when she turned 15. After auditioning for ABC Paramount Records, she impressed legendary record producer Don Costa, who subsequently signed her.

However, success didn't come easy for Carole, as her first few singles failed to make an impact. It was also during this time that she created her stage name, Carole King.

As she was still writing songs and developing her skills at the young age of 16, Carole became a student at Queens College in New York City. While there, she met Gerry Goffin, another music lover and aspiring lyricist. With mutual passions, the two began to write songs together and fell in love. Their romance grew quickly, and at 17, Carole became pregnant with their first child, a daughter, Louise. The two got married shortly afterward, in August 1959.

With a baby and a goal to make it big in songwriting, the couple dropped out of school, took day jobs, and wrote songs well into the evening. The two wrote for Aldon Music when songwriters were continuously writing one song after another, hoping one of them would become their big break.

Luckily for Carole and Gerry, they finally got their hit with "Will You Love Me Tomorrow." Performed by The Shirelles, the song is about a woman asking the man she's with if, after spending the night together, will he still want to be with her in the morning. The song became an incredible success, reaching number one on the Billboard Hot 100 chart and making history as the first Black female group to hit the number one spot. The accomplishment was staggering, and feeling like they finally reached success, Carole and Gerry quit their day jobs to become full-time songwriters.

In a Boys Club

After finally getting their hit song, the chart-topping singles for Carole and Gerry didn't stop. The music of the 60s was booming, and Carole and Gerry were dominating the charts with their songs "Chains," "The Loco-Motion," "Keep Your Hands Off My Baby," and "One Fine Day," to name a few. Numerous artists, including The Beatles, The Monkees, and Dusty Springfield, sang their songs. Yet, it wasn't until their stratosphere-hitting song, "(You Make Me Feel Like) A Natural Woman," sung by Aretha Franklin, made Carole and Gerry, two of the most popular and in-demand songwriters.

Although Carole's career was hitting all the high notes, her personal life was falling flat. In social settings, she realized she stood out. All the women around her were housewives, filling domestic roles and becoming mothers. While being a mother herself, having a successful and demanding job on top of it is something society deems only a man should fill. Even more so, she was working in a male-dominated industry. Having a woman writing songs from a female perspective, instead of men telling women what their ideals of life should be, is out of the ordinary. Luckily, at least in her work, she was unbothered by being one of the very few women, remembering her parents always telling her she could be whomever she wanted, and nothing should stop her.

Nevertheless, her choice of mixing business with pleasure became troublesome as well. Gerry began having numerous affairs, misusing drugs, and was diagnosed as bipolar. In 1968, Carole and Gerry divorced. Carole then moved with their two daughters, Louise and Sherry, to Los Angeles and began a new chapter in her career.

In Front of the Microphone

Los Angeles was becoming the new 'it' city for the recording industry. After her move, Carole joined a group of songwriters, including James Taylor, Joni Mitchell, and Toni Stern. She developed close friendships with James and Tony in particular, and they helped her form her own voice within her songwriting without Gerry.

Alongside her growth as a songwriter, Carole forms a group with musicians Charles Lorkley (her soon-to-be second husband) and Danny Kortchmar, called The City. The trio makes an album but disbands shortly after due to lack of promotion and Carole's stage fright.

Nevertheless, the setback didn't stop Carole. In the early 60s, she released singles "Baby Sittin'" and "It Might as Well Rain Until September," which fared pretty well on the U.S. and British charts. Still, songwriting was her main focus, and she put singing on the back burner. But something about being in a new environment with new inspiration, Carole took the singer-songwriter plunge and released her first solo album, Writer, in May 1970.

Writer features renditions of her own songs she had other artists record, including "Up on the Roof" and "Child of Mine." The album received mixed reviews and performed low on the charts, peaking at 84 on the Billboard Top 200.

Once again, Carole didn't let failure hold her back, and with the support of James, she began working on her record-breaking second album.

Tapestry

Carole's second album, Tapestry, was released on February 10, 1971. It only took three weeks to record. It featured brand new songs and another round of her rendition of her hit songs made famous by other artists. "(You Make Me Feel Like) A Natural Woman" and "Will You Love Me Tomorrow" are included as slowed-down piano ballads compared to their pop and soul counterparts.

While the album was packed full of masterpieces, standouts on the album include "I Feel the Earth Move," a song about the feelings she has when her lover is around. Her award-winning single, "It's Too Late," tackles the realization that her relationship is coming to an end, while "You've Got a Friend" discusses loyalty.

The album was unique regarding the synchronization of her vocals and the accompanying instruments. It's in the way the listener feels the emotion in the songs, not only through the way Carole sings but also in the way instruments compliment her. The excitement in Carole's voice in "I Feel the Earth Move " is reciprocated with the notes on the piano. When she sings that, she feels herself "tumbling down," the piano sounds like it's tumbling with her.

Furthermore, Carole took a new approach to women creating music, not only as a singer but as a songwriter, too. She tells relatable stories in her lyrics that resonate with women. Additionally, the production of the album is raw and less polished compared to the pop sound of the time.

Carole's unique approach to Tapestry paid off as the world fell in love with the album. Selling over 25 million copies worldwide, it stayed in the number one position on the Billboard charts for a record-breaking 15 weeks, along with staying on the charts in different positions for over six years.

The continuous success and record-breaking of Tapestry didn't seem to end. At the 1972 Grammy Awards, Carole took home the awards for Album of the Year and Best Pop Vocal Performance for a female. She also became the first woman to win Song of the Year for "You've Got a Friend," and the first solo female artist to win Record of the Year for "It's Too Late."

Years after the Grammys, the legacy of Tapestry continued. The album has continuously appeared on 'best of' lists, was inducted into the Grammy Hall of Fame in 1998, became the best-selling album by a female artist for 25 years, and was added to the National Recording Registry at the Library of Congress to be preserved for its cultural impact on the United States.

If there was any question about Carole's talent or her ability to break some of the glass ceilings in the music industry, her track record of success says otherwise.

Now and Forever

Carole was still riding on the phenomenal success of Tapestry with the release of Music in December of 1971. Music continues with the same musical style of mellow sounds and main piano accompaniment, and she once again teams up with Toni to write the songs "Too Much Rain" and the single "It's Going to Take Some Time." The album was a success, selling well over half a million copies in its first week. And, as if releasing two albums in the same year wasn't enough, she kept the momentum going. With Rhymes and Reasons in October 1972 and Fantasy in June 1973, the former going platinum and the latter going gold.

In 1973, Carole was at the height of her fame as a musician, and in an act that kicked her stage fight out the door, she performed a free concert in Central Park to over 100,000 fans.

Then, in September 1974, she released her sixth record, Wrap Around Joy. The album was followed by the 1976 release of Thoroughbred, featuring well-known singer-songwriters David Crosby and Graham Nash. Carole once again worked with James and surprisingly wrote four songs with Gerry.

After Thoroughbred's clutch on popularity was loosening, Carole divorced Charles and moved with her four children to Idaho.

In Idaho, Carole fell in love with the beautiful mountain and forest landscape around her and became an environmental activist. Over the years, she joined the Alliance for the Wild Rockies. She even went in front of Congress on multiple occasions in support of the Northern Rockies Ecosystem Protection Act.

Her second love since moving to Idaho is Rick Evers. He became her songwriting partner for the record Simple Things in July 1977, and the two married shortly after. However, the success of the album and her professional relationship with her husband didn't translate well into her personal life. Rick became abusive towards Carole and died of a drug overdose not long after their marriage.

A Different Tune

Going into the 1980s and the 1990s, Carole took different opportunities in her career. She released a few more albums through the years, but her sound didn't match the synth-pop of the 80s or the grunge rock of the 90s, resulting in lacklustre success compared to her previous work.

During the two decades, she provided songs for movie soundtracks such as The Care Bears Movie, A League of Their Own, and You Got Mail. Carole even dabbled in acting and appeared in the Broadway play Blood Brothers.

It was also during this time that Carole received recognition for her contributions to the music industry. In 1987, she was inducted into the Songwriters Hall of Fame, followed by her and Gerry receiving the National Academy of Songwriters' Lifetime Achievement Award. Finally, in 1990, she and Gerry were inducted into the Rock and Roll Hall of Fame for songwriting.

It's All Looking Beautiful

In the 2000s, Carole still wasn't slowing down. If anything, she kept proving her unbreakable power within the music industry. In 2000, she re-recorded her song "Where You Lead" from Tapestry for the theme song of the TV drama Gilmore Girls. With the help of her daughter, Louise, Carole updated the lyrics' theme of being loyal to one man, to the bond between a mother and daughter, and female friendships. Carole was proud of the updated version of "Where You Lead," as she no longer felt a connection to the song since she originally wrote it back in 1971.

She released the album Love Makes the World in 2001. The album consists of her interpretations of songs she gave to other artists like Celine Dion, Steven Tyler, and K.D. Lang, in the 90s.

A few years after the album's release, Carole went on the Living Room Tour in July 2004, making stops in the United States, Canada, New Zealand, and Australia. Carole released an accompanying live album that broke the Billboard Top 20 chart.

After finishing the Living Room Tour, she toured Japan with modern artists Fergie and Mary J. Blige, a wild combination that performed exceptionally well.

In 2007, she returned to the Troubadour stage with James Taylor to celebrate the nightclub's 50th anniversary, while also reminiscing their first time performing there together in the early 70s. Their shows at the Troubadour were constant sell-outs, and they decided to extend their show to a world tour.

The two long-time friends embarked on the Troubadour Reunion Tour in 2010, a widely successful tour that became one of the high-earning concerts of the year. Accompanying the tour was the Live at the Troubadour album, selling millions of copies and debuting at number four on Billboard.

Now well into her 70s, the concept of Carole retiring is non-existent. She released her New York

Times bestselling biography, A Natural Woman, in 2012, along with receiving a star on the Hollywood Walk of Fame.

2013 proved to be a big year of accomplishments for Carole. She received The Recording Academy Lifetime Achievement Award and became the first woman to be presented the Library of Congress Gershwin Prize for Popular Song.

A Broadway play about her life and career, entitled Beautiful: The Carole King Musical, began its debut to intense popularity and won two Tony Awards and a Grammy. The musical's success launched tours around the world, even receiving two Olivier Awards in London.

In 2021, Carole made history once more. She was inducted into the Rock and Roll Hall of Fame for a second time as a singer. Her achievement marks the first time an artist has been inducted separately as a singer and a songwriter.

When looking at her entire career, Carole's accolades have no limits. Over 1,000 artists have recorded compositions from her 400-song catalogue and over 100 chart-topping singles. Leaving no question, she's one of, if not the most successful female singer-songwriters on the planet.

Chapter 3: Chrissie Hynde

In the 1970s, music was evolving rapidly. From the emergence of the singer-songwriter, glam rock, and disco, the music industry was thriving in ways it never achieved in previous decades. Filled with excess, 70s mainstream music was a money-making machine. The commercialization from concerts, record sales, and merchandise exceeded an artist's wildest dreams of fame and fortune. While the beginning of the decade saw musicians focus on their integrity and the stories they wanted to tell, the mid to late 70s had artists throwing their morals out the window in favour of popularity and millions of dollars.

While everything seemed to be at ease, there were whispers about an emerging rock genre in New York, going back to basics with guitars and drums but louder, assertive, and a lot less polished. The full-fledged arrival of punk came with a bang instead of a whisper and challenged the status quo of the current music scene.

Punk grew out of the 60s garage rock scene, with main credit going to Iggy Pop and his band The Stooges. The music had no order; the classically trained and professionalism of most artists in previous decades didn't apply. These new artists didn't know the rules, so it was easy to break them.

Not only was punk breaking the rules. It was an act of rebellion. Punk bands didn't believe in the 60s hippie 'everything is love' and 'everything is fine' aesthetic because things were not fine. The youth was sick of compliance, feeling like they had to follow in their parent's footsteps and listening to watered-down music that didn't express how they felt.

As punk music became popular, it thrived in New York with The Ramones and the New York Dolls, but it really took dominance in London, not only as a music genre but as a lifestyle. The Sex Pistols and The Clash were dominating, and everywhere you looked, there was someone with spiked multi-coloured hair, a leather jacket, a spiked belt, and combat boots. Punk was pure anti-establishment towards the government, societal norms, and the past state of the music industry.

So, who could blame a young woman from small-town America—who lived and breathed everything punk—for packing her bags and moving to London?

But just like every other aspect of the music industry, punk was dominated by men, and unsurprisingly, there was hardly a woman in sight.

Even so, the punk scene thrived on disrupting societal norms, and nothing could disrupt the establishment more than a woman who wouldn't take no for an answer when told she couldn't create her own music. And that woman was Chrissie Hynde.

When I Change My Life

Christine Ellen Hynde was born on September 7, 1951, in Akron, Ohio, to parents Melville and Dolores. As a child, Chrissie's dad worked for the Marine Corps before switching jobs to work for the Ohio Bell Telephone Company, with the Hyndes moving wherever his career needed him.

Moving from Akron to Cleveland and back to Akron, Chrissie's childhood was safe and basic. She hated it. Chrissie hated how every day was exactly the same as the last and the cookie-cutter lifestyle every family lived. She wanted excitement. She wanted adventure. As Chrissie grew, she became rebellious and reckless, even scaring her classmates for her own amusement.

At Litchfield Junior High School, Chrissie met Nita Lee. The two became inseparable with their non-conforming attitudes and lifestyle. The girls didn't like or care for the popular music at the time, passing classes, or dating. Instead, Chrissie and Nita fell more in love with the underground rock scene, disenfranchised themselves more, started taking drugs and hating on the older generations for their racism and wars.

At 15, Chrissie realized she wanted more in life and was tired of small-town living; she wanted to leave and see the world.

But at quite a young age, Chrissie knew she couldn't leave just yet, so instead, she followed around local bands and began to play guitar to ease the need for adventure.

One night, at Chippewa Lake Park, Chrissie watches Mitch Ryder and the Detroit Wheels play. Halfway through their set, a fight broke out on stage, and Chrissie became mesmerized at how the bandmates' fighting seemed to match the raw and organic sounds of the music they were playing as if it was a visual performance.

After the band finished, another one took to the stage, and again, halfway through their playing, Chrissie noticed things getting tense between the band members, and they too started fighting. Chrissie realized that all the yelling and fist throwing was staged. While the violence might turn others off, Chrissie loved it and decided her new goal in life was to join a band.

Girl in the Band

Chrissie was ambitious and went on the hunt to form a band. Miraculously, she graduated high school, attended Kent State University to study art, and finally formed a band, Sat Sun Mat. Unfortunately, the band wouldn't be her claim to fame, and after three years at university, Chrissie dropped out. In 1973, the London punk scene was calling her, so she packed her bags and moved to London.

Finally, out and experiencing the world, Chrissie was set on finding a job. She worked random odd jobs before putting her art education to good use and got hired at an architectural firm. She didn't stay long, as she got fired after a few months. During her downtime, she went to a pub with her friend and rock critic, Nick Kent, who offered her a job being a music journalist at NME. Chrissie took the job but quit shortly after as she believed she wasn't good at it; even though she was getting notoriety for her work, she didn't want her recognition to be as a rock journalist.

Not one to be jobless for long, Chrissie found a new job that was right up her alley at the clothing store, SEX, a boutique owned by fashion designers Vivienne Westwood and Malcolm McLaren that became the pinnacle clothing store for punk fashion. Chrissie was right in the punk scene. Sid Vicious, who eventually rose to fame in the Sex Pistols, worked at the store too. But once again, regardless of how deep into the scene she was, her plans to get a band off the ground fail. However, her connections were good, and she received a phone call with an offer to sing in a band; the catch is that the band was in France. Unwavering in her goal to see her dream as a reality, she packed up her belongings and moved once more.

Chrissie joined the Frenchies but believed the band offered nothing unique to the punk music sound and spontaneously moved back to Cleveland. Once she's back in the state of Ohio, her work opportunities weren't so great either. She worked with the R&B group Jack Rabbit, helping them form the sound of their music, but when money got tight, Chrissie flew back to Paris in 1976.

Back in France, Chrissie grew frustrated as those around her formed bands and signed record deals while she was still struggling. Looking for any solution, she teams up with her old boss Malcolm. In a desperate attempt, Malcolm suggested Chrissie cut off all her hair and dress like a man to join a band called Loverboys. She refused, and he moved her to another band to just play guitar. Again, unimpressed, Malcolm had her join Dave Vanian, Chris Millar, and Ray Burns to form Masters of the Backside. Chaos in her new band ensues as Dave doesn't want to perform live, and Malcolm is too busy managing the Sex Pistols, which resulted in Ray and Chris forming the successful punk band The Damned and abandoning Chrissie.

Feeling defeated but still determined to reach her goals, she connected with a band manager named Tony Secunda. She performed her song, "The Phone Call," for him, and seeing her talent as a musician and songwriter offered her studio time so she could form a band and make some demos.

Chrissie made a demo of "The Phone Call" and gave it to Dave Hill, owner of Real Records. Dave enjoyed her demo, but her backing band isn't the right fit, so Chrissie and Dave scouted for musicians. Eventually, they found Pete Farndon, James Honeyman-Scott, and Martin Chambers to form The Pretenders.

Finally, Chrissie had her band.

Brass in Pocket

The Pretender's first single, "Stop Your Sobbing," is a harmonic, hold-no-punches cover of a Kinks single. The song made it onto the Top 40 charts in the United Kingdom, followed by "Kid" and their number one single, "Brass in Pocket."

Their self-titled first album was released on December 27, 1979, to mass commercial and critical success for their new wave, punk-pop sound. As Chrissie was finally doing what she always dreamed of, she and the rest of the band wasted no time to record their second album, Extended Play, on March 30, 1981, with chart-toppers "Talk of the Town" and "Message of Love." The same year, the band released Pretenders II on August 15, which also became a success.

While everything for the band seemed great from the outside, behind closed doors, trouble was brewing as the early 80s gave Chrissie many hardships. She and Pete began a relationship in 1979, which came to an end in 1981 when Chrissie started a relationship with the Kinks lead singer, Ray Davies, and the couple had a daughter, Natalie Rae Hynde, in 1980. When her relationship with Pete ended, his use of alcohol and drugs increased, resulting in his live performances becoming unpredictable and being fired by Chrissie after completing their world tour on June 14, 1982. Just days after the firing, James died of a cocaine overdose. Now dealing with the loss of two band members, she debated asking Pete to return, but Martin decided against it. Unfortunately, Pete would die in 1983 of his own drug overdose, leaving Chrissie and Martin, the surviving members of The Pretenders.

Don't Get Me Wrong

Not wanting the music to die after the deaths of Pete and James, Chrissie and Martin carried on. Adding temporary replacements, the band recorded the song "Back on the Chain Gang," a song Chrissie wrote as a tribute and to process the death of James. The song was a success, reaching the top ten charts in the U.S. and the U.K.

Out of the success of recording the single, the band recruited Robbie McIntosh as the lead guitar player and Malcolm Foster for bass. With the new line-up, The Pretenders began to record their third album, Learning to Crawl. Released on January 1, 1984, the album peaked at number five on the Billboard Top 200, and along with "Back on the Chain Gang," the singles "My City was Gone," a story of Chrissie visiting her hometown of Akron and seeing the development and changes that took place since she left; and "200 Miles," which became a popular Christmas song due to the mention of the holiday.

Riding off the success of Learning to Crawl, the band was in the process of making another album when another line-up change happened. Chrissie and Martin were trying their best to process their grief over the death of the two bandmates; they were both struggling. Chrissie with her creativity and Martin with his drumming. Realizing she's come too far for the band to fall apart; Chrissie made the tough decision to fire Martin from the band.

However, not everything is bad. Chrissie married Simple Minds lead singer Jim Kerr in 1984, and a year later, Chrissie gave birth to her second daughter, Yasmin. Nonetheless, Chrissie and Jim divorced in 1990.

By the time the band's next album is released, 1986, Get Close, Chrissie was the only original member. Once again, she used session musicians before adding T.M. Stevens and Blair Cunningham to the band.

It was not until 1990 that The Pretenders released a new album, Packed! However, there were no official band members except for Chrissie, as she kicked T.M. and Blair out of the band for not seeing eye to eye on her creative vision for the band.

On May 9, 1994, the album Last of the Independents was released, with Martin returning to the band. The album performed well and featured the smash hit ballad, "I'll Stand by You." During the mid to late 90s, Chrissie branched out from The Pretenders. She recorded the song "Luck Be a Lady" with Frank Sinatra for his album Duets II in 1994 and acted in an episode of the legendary show Friends, returning to her work with The Pretenders for 1999's Viva El Amor.

In the 2000s, the band released Loose Screw in 2002, with the same members of Last of the Independents, making the most consistent line-up since the deaths of Pete and James. Break Up the Concrete was released on October 7, 2008, without Martin, due to creative differences. Alone was released in 2016 and once again consisted of a backing band, with Chrissie being the sole member.

Talk of the Town

If Chrissie can be known for anything, it's her stubbornness and willingness to get what she wants, exactly how she wants it, and she won't let anyone get in her way.

In a career spanning over 40 years, 70-year-old Chrissie has no plans of slowing down. She finally became more comfortable having her name on the cover of an album, releasing her first solo record, Stockholm, in 2014 to great success, a collaborative album with the Valve Bone Woe Ensemble, entitled Valve Bone Woe in 2019, and in 2021 Standing in the Doorway: Chrissie Hynde Sings Bob Dylan.

Chrissie also added author to her resume, releasing her autobiography, Reckless: My Life as a Pretender, in 2015.

In 2021, she reunited with The Pretenders—Martin included—and released the album Hate for Sale to favourable reviews.

Over the years, she became known to be quite vocal about her opinions. Being a vegetarian for decades, she has never been quiet about her love of animals and animal rights, even getting arrested in France for smearing blood on a KFC. She's also expressed her dislike for award shows, especially the Grammys. Even when she was inducted into the Rock 'n Roll Hall of Fame with The Pretenders, she described it as the most un-rock 'n roll thing to do.

In an interview with The Guardian in 2016, when asked about her career, Chrissie said, "If they like my music, that's great, turn on the radio. If they don't like it, switch it off. I have no other message, other than vegetarianism, which has always been exactly the same thing I said right from day one."

Now, what could be more punk than that.

Chapter 4: Dolly Parton

The year is 1973, and Dolly Parton has a lot on her mind. She's in her house, her papers in front of her, ready to write for her songwriting session. Soon enough, she's finished writing two songs, one about the time a female bank teller hit on her husband shortly after they got married, and the second expressing how she was going to tell her friend and music partner Porter Wagoner that she had to leave his show and form her own career path.

Her songwriting session proved to be quite rewarding. The latter song completed her separation from Porter, who finally understood it was beyond overdue for her to leave. And the former song was received well by her record company; it even became the title of her thirteenth studio album.

When the album was released in 1974, the success of the two songs was unimaginable. Not only did they perform well on the charts, but they also became two of Dolly's signature songs, leaving a massive impact on country music and pop culture. The effect is still felt to this day, as artists have recorded their own versions of the songs since their release.

In 2018, Dolly revealed that she wrote the songs on the same day, leaving fans and critics floored and how impeccable her talent is.

So, what were the two songs? Well, they were "Jolene" and "I Will Always Love You."

Just the Way I Am

Born on January 19, 1946, Dolly Rebecca Parton became the fourth out of twelve children to Avie Lee Caroline and Robert Lee Parton Sr in Pittman Centre, Tennessee. Living on a small farm for such a big family, the Partons worked hard but lived in poverty, with such common necessities as electricity and running water being a luxury.

Her paternal side of the family were born-bred farmers, working hard in the hope of good pay to support their family. Dolly's maternal side of the family was the polar opposite. They focused on living one day at a time, carefree, and singing songs without a moment's thought of making a living. However, Avie and Robert made it work. Regardless of how tough it was, Robert was determined to provide for his wife and children, while Avie taught Dolly and her siblings to sing folklore songs. Their personalities provided Dolly with a balance of hard work and creativity.

Dolly's perspective on life became a mix of both of her parents; as a young child, she worked hard on her skills as a musician. Dolly wrote her first song at the age of 7. Growing up religious, she would practice her singing skills in front of her community at Sunday church services, and at 8, one of her maternal uncles, Bill Owens, bought her her first guitar.

Realizing her skills, Bill introduced her to the local radio station personality and entrepreneur who gave Dolly her first broadcasting performance on The Cas Walker Farm and Home Hour in Knoxville.

Being a mainstay on the show, Dolly grew her connections in the local music scene and landed a slot performing with Bill at the Grand Ole Opry at 13. Their performance garnered three encores. Following her Grand Ole Opry performance, Dolly recorded the single "Puppy Love" on a local Louisiana label, Goldband Records. The single didn't perform well, but it helped Dolly learn more about the music industry and the process of recording music.

Once Dolly graduated high school in 1964, along with being the first person in her family to do so, she knew her aspirations were too big for her small town, and she moved to Nashville the next day.

Blonde Ambition

When she arrived in Nashville, Dolly immediately sprang into action so she could get her music career going. She also met the love of her life within the first few days of being in Nashville. Carl Dean ran a road-paving business in the city; he and Dolly quickly fell in love and married in 1966.

Her first break in the Nashville music scene came as a songwriter in collaboration with her uncle Bill. Singing with Monument Records, label heads wanted Dolly to sing pop and rockabilly songs, but Dolly refused, being adamant that she was a country singer. Not wanting her to go down the country route, the label focused on her songwriting talents instead. However, when country singer Bill Phillips began to record her song, "Put It Off Till Tomorrow," he asked her to sing the harmony. The song became a country hit and, uncredited for her contribution, listeners and the record label became curious about who the female singing on the track was. Dolly revealed to her label that it was her voice, and her label finally agreed that she should record country music.

Dolly released her first album, Hello, I'm Dolly, on February 13, 1967. The album contained the singles "Dumb Blonde" and "A Something Fishy," both performed well on the country music charts. The record also grew Dolly's mainstream popularity, catching the attention of Porter Wagoner, a man who would significantly impact the following years in Dolly's career.

Second Best

Porter hosted the weekly television show, The Porter Wagoner Show, a half an hour weekly variety show that featured Dolly and Porter performing songs together and special guests. Once Dolly joined, the show grew in its immense popularity, becoming the number one TV show in America.

As recognition of Dolly grew thanks to the show, Portner knew that Dolly's talent needed to be showcased outside of the program, so he convinced his label, RCA Victor, to sign her. RCA Victor did, with the condition that Dolly and Porter recorded a duet. The two singers covered Tom Paxton's "The Last Thing on My Mind," which reached the Top 10 on the country charts. They subsequently released Just Between You and Me in 1968, the first album out of 12 Dolly would record with Porter and 13 solo albums while on his show.

The same year, Dolly released her second album, Just Because I'm a Woman, featuring songs with lyrics quite ahead of its time. With the title track about a woman calling out her lover's hypocrisy in criticizing her for having sex with other men before their relationship even though he did the same.

Her following nine albums feature similar storytelling in her lyrics, with standouts including 1971s "Coat of Many Colours," off the album of the same name, the song about growing up in poverty. The song covers the time when Dolly attended a school that had picture day. Her mother made her a coat out of different quilt patterns, and while Dolly loved it, her classmates bullied her for wearing a weird jacket with no shirt underneath.

While Dolly's solo albums were praised critically, they were overshadowed by her singles and albums with Porter. During the early to mid-70s, Dolly became frustrated with the lack of praise for her solo work. With tensions between her and Porter rising, Dolly began thinking it was time for her to end their business relationship.

Additionally, Porter was becoming possessive and verbally abusive towards Dolly. He started to dictate what and how she should sing, telling her to shut up during a 1973 episode and pushed her uncle Bill out of her business collaborations.

Eventually, Dolly had enough and expressed to Porter it was time for her to leave, which he adamantly ignored. Unsure how to get her decision through to him, she decided writing a song was the best option.

Dolly wrote "I Will Always Love You" and sang it to Porter the day after she wrote it. Porter, in tears, finally heard Dolly and agreed to have her leave the show, with his one condition that he produce the song for release.

Finally, Dolly was free.

9-5

Free to create whatever music she wanted; Dolly decided she wanted her music to have more mainstream appeal by crossing over into pop. So, she made the creative decision that the music she released going forward had a pop/country sound.

Things started out rocky until her 1977 album, Here You Come Again, became certified platinum and performed well on the Billboard Country charts and Billboard 200. Dolly even won a Grammy in 1978 for Best Female Country Vocal Performance for the album.

Dolly continued with two more albums in the 70s, Heartbreaker in 1978 and Great Balls of Fire in 1979; both releases performed highly on the charts.

With her star rising, she made appearances on TV screens in specials, including one of her own with Carol Burnett.

By the time the 80s arrived, Dolly was ready to add another credential to her resume, this time as an actress.

Hollywood is Calling

In 1980, Dolly made her acting debut in 9 to 5, an ensemble cast with Lily Tomlin and Jane Fonda. The plot follows three women who seek revenge and dismantle the workplace of their sexist and narcissistic boss. While it's Dolly's first movie, it is not the first time she was offered a movie role, as she only accepted the part of Doralee because Jane wanted her specifically.

Dolly recorded the theme song to the movie, "9-5," and it became a smash hit, reaching number one on Billboard, along with receiving an Academy Award nomination for Best Original Song. In promotional events for the song, Dolly revealed she used her infamous acrylic nails as an instrument to create rhythm and harmony; her nails even got a credit in the song's liner notes.

After the success of the movie and the theme song, Dolly released her first concept album, "9 to 5 and Odd Jobs," reaching gold status and number one on the Billboard Country chart. The success of an album dedicated to working pays off, and Dolly won two Grammys for Best Female Country Vocal Performance and Best Country Song.

If the accolades for the album weren't enough, it's clear Dolly has a natural talent for acting, as she received two Golden Globe nominations.

Her next film is the musical, The Best Little Whorehouse in Texas in 1982. The film performed well at the box office, and she once again received a Golden Globe nomination for Best Actress in a Motion Picture (Comedy or Musical). Dolly stars in other films, but they don't reach the same success as her first two until 1989's Steel Magnolias.

Regardless of how time-consuming a film schedule is, Dolly still didn't slow down in her music output, releasing an album every year of the 80s except for 1981, 1986, and 1988.

However, her triumph in acting and music during this time didn't come without difficulties. She was ridiculed for her weight while starring in The Best Little Whorehouse in Texas and personally struggled when she had a hysterectomy brought on by endometriosis. While she and Carl never have children as a result, she accepted the procedure well as the couple helped raise her nieces and nephews throughout the years.

Despite a few upsets, the 80s treat Dolly nicely. She even adds businesswoman to her repertoire, opening her theme park, Dollywood, in Sevier County, and she is inducted into the Nashville Songwriters Hall of Fame.

Working Girl

In the 1990s, most of Dolly's achievements came from behind the scenes. Whitney Houston covered "I Will Always Love You" for the soundtrack of her 1992 film, The Bodyguard, and the song skyrocketed on the charts and in sales, with the publishing rights having Dolly laughing to the bank.

She released ten albums in the 90s and ventured into bluegrass with the 1999 album The Grass is Blue and won the Grammy for Best Bluegrass Album. That same year she was inducted into the Country Music Hall of Fame.

Going into the 2000s, Dolly released her second bluegrass album, Little Sparrow, in 2001. The release of the two bluegrass albums is monumental for Dolly, as they once again showcased her versatility in multiple music genres. They are released on Dolly's record label, Blue Eye Records.

In 2005, she received another Academy Award nomination for Best Original Song with "Travelin' Thru," that she wrote specifically for the Transamerica soundtrack. The film, about a trans mother going on a road trip across the country with her son, sparked controversy with some of Dolly's fan base to the point she received death threats.

However, nothing could stop Dolly, and she continued thriving. In 2007, Dolly created her second record label, Dolly Records, where she has and still currently publishes her albums. In 2014, she released her 42nd album, Blue Smoke, topping the charts around the globe and becoming her first top 10 album.

Following the album's success, she embarked on two world tours, the first being for Blue Smoke and the second for 2016's Pure and Simple. Moreover, she proved that age has nothing to do with her career, as she played Glastonbury Festival to over 1800,000 fans at the age of 68.

Dolly even took on more business opportunities when in 2015, she announced she was creating a production company, Dixie Pixie Productions. Shortly after the announcement, she released Dolly Parton's

Heartstrings in 2019, an anthology series that tells the origin stories of her most popular songs.

You're in Dollywood Now

At the age of 75, Dolly has zero plans for retirement. She's a force to be reckoned with by selling over 100 million records, 11 Grammy Awards, a Lifetime Achievement Award, and writing over 3,000 songs.

Aside from her success in the music business, her notoriety comes from her personality and generosity. The former comes from her quick wit and humour, so well known, it's called 'Dollyisms."

Her generosity, on the other hand, makes her more loveable by the public. She founded the Dollywood Foundation in 1988, promising $500 to students who graduate seventh and eighth grade, resulting in a significant change in dropout rates from 36% to 6%. Furthermore, she has her Imagination Library, providing millions of free books to children around the world.

And, if it wasn't possible to love her anymore, she donated $1 million to the Vanderbilt University Medical Centre for COVID-19 vaccine research.

Clearly, this is Dolly's world. We're just living in it.

Chapter 5: Stevie Nicks

It's May 23, 1997, at the Warner Bros. Studios in Burbank, California. The auditorium was packed to the brim with Hollywood A-listers for an event that was a surprise when it was announced.

The band set to take the stage is legendary, breaking world records and having resonating hit singles and albums that have been influential to artists since their release. However, the band's five members haven't performed together as a complete unit since the late 80s. To say the live show was a must-see is an understatement.

The band was Fleetwood Mac.

Reaching superstar status in the mid-1970s, the band dealt with a lot of in-fighting over the years, resulting in bandmates Stevie Nicks, Lindsey Buckingham, and Christine McVie leaving the band over different periods of time.

When the trio left, they still kept in touch with each other and the two remaining band members to help with solo work. However, when MTV executives approached them for an MTV Unplugged special, the five decided to reunite.

Deciding to make the best of the event, Fleetwood Mac made the decision to perform their biggest hits and perform two new songs; "Bleed to Love Her" and "My Little Demon."

Once Fleetwood Mac took the stage, their performance was electric; the vocal harmony and instrumentation were so on point one would never guess there was ever any turmoil. Their cohesiveness and love of music and songwriting shone, proving why

44

they're the most successful line-up and deserving of their fame.

While there's no argument that each member of the band performed to their best, it's Stevie who stands out. She sang with such fierceness, and when the band played the songs specifically about her relationship with Lindsey, she sang directly at him, audience be damned. Additionally, she performed with her signature witchy ways: a long black dress, dancing in circles, and waving her arms in the air.

Following the success of the show, Fleetwood Mac released a live album of the show, The Dance. The album reached number one on the charts, their first since 1987's Tango in the Night and became the fifth best-selling live album of all time. Once again solidifying that the addition of Lindsey and Stevie lead to the band becoming legendary.

Dreams

Born to parents Barbara Alice Meeks and Aaron Jess Seth Nicks Jr., Stephanie Lynn Nicks entered the world on May 26, 1948, in Phoenix, Arizona. Her upbringing was quite comfortable, as her father was an avid businessman who rose the corporate ladder in different high-profile jobs. In her childhood, her paternal grandfather, Aaron Jess Nicks, or A.J. as he's commonly known, played music locally, and when he visited Stevie, he sang to her. When Stevie turned 4, he began to teach her how to sing.

Nonetheless, Aaron began to achieve multiple promotions at numerous high-profile jobs, keeping the family always on the move across the United States. Because of the constant relocations, Stevie realized that the friendships she made were fleeting, so she spent her time learning piano, drawing, and dancing. Throughout her performance training in the 1950s and

1960s, Stevie was always listening to the radio. Eventually, her parents realized her love of music wasn't just a hobby and bought her a guitar for her 15th birthday.

A year later, Stevie got her moment of realization that music was the career choice for her. After her boyfriend broke up with her so he could date her friend, a heartbroken Stevie ran to her room. Guitar, pen, and notebook in hand, she wrote her first song, titled "I've Loved and I've Lost, and I'm Sad but I'm Not Blue." After writing the song, she sang it to herself and realized that songwriting and performing songs is her career path.

Peace, Love, and Rock n Roll

Now in California, thanks to her father's new job, Stevie was still adamant about music. She went to a local church that offered night music jam sessions and ended up recognizing a boy from her high school, Lindsey Buckingham. He played "California Dreamin'" by The Mamas & the Papas. Since Stevie knew and liked the song, she made the bold decision to join his performance. Their duet went over well, but it would be over a year before Stevie would collaborate with Lindsey again. During his time without Stevie, Lindsey played guitar and bass in the band Fritz. As the band grew in popularity, Lindsey realized they could become successful. But with repeated failures, bandmates started to leave. Lindsey decided the best solution was to add a female singer, and he remembered Stevie.

Lindsey contacted Stevie to audition, and she agreed. Her audition stands out, and she became the lead singer of Fritz. As the new formation of the band performed gigs to promote themselves, they ended up getting a booking agent who helped them perform shows in different venues in California.

As Fritz gained more recognition, the band became frustrated that Stevie became the star. When Fritz performed, and the announcer said the names of the musicians, they received polite applause. But when Stevie was announced, she'd receive cheers from the crowd. Things became more complicated within the band when Stevie and Lindsey began a romantic relationship in 1966.

Eventually, the band's manager knew that Stevie and Lindsey were the standouts, and the remaining band was holding them back. He told them they could be successful in music together and connected them with Keith Olsen, a chief engineer for a small recording studio. The two made the decision to dissolve the band and work with Keith. Stevie and Lindsey recorded their first and only album as a duo, "Buckingham Nicks," in 1973. The album was an utter failure, resulting in Stevie and Lindsey having to pick up odd jobs to make money. It was during this time Stevie discovered cocaine while she was cleaning a house. As it wasn't seen as a harmful drug, Stevie began to use it frequently, resulting in an addiction lasting for over a decade.

Just as things seemed to be going downhill for Stevie and Lindsey, Mick Fleetwood randomly heard the Buckingham Nicks album. As the drummer of the band Fleetwood Mac, his band was going through a line-up change and needed a guitarist. Impressed with Lindsey's skills as a guitarist, Mick reached out and asked him to join the band. Lindsey told Mick the only way he'd join Mick's band is if they added Stevie too, as they were a package deal. Mick agreed to Lindsey's terms after a dinner at a Mexican restaurant with the rest of the band, Christine and John McVie.

Lindsey and Stevie joined Fleetwood Mac in 1974, with Mick not realizing the level of success his band was about to achieve with the two musicians.

Stop Draggin' My Heart Around

Once Stevie and Lindsey were in the band, they were rapidly turning out songs. Stevie contributed the songs "Landslide," "Crystal," and "Rihannon" to the self-titled album. Fleetwood Mac was released on July 11, 1975, but it wasn't until the band went on tour that the album started to rise on the charts, with Stevie's "Rhiannon" being one of their top ten songs.

It was during this time when the band became part of the 70s rock and roll party lifestyle. Alcohol, cocaine, and pot surrounded the band everywhere they went. Their long nights of partying turned into early mornings, and Fleetwood Mac eventually became known as one of the heaviest party bands in rock music. Stevie even revealed in later years that she probably spent over $1 million on cocaine for herself, the band, and others.

After the constant touring for the self-titled album, Stevie decided it was time to end her romantic relationship with Lindsey. Prior to joining Fleetwood Mac, the two had difficulties but worked through their issues and focused on the band and album. When the couple has a big fight after a show, Stevie calls it quits but says neither of them would leave the band, and they would put their differences aside for the sake of the music.

Following the success of the album and tour, the band was pressured to record a successful follow-up. However, Stevie and Lindsey weren't the only band members to have relationship issues. Christine and John, who were married for eight years, were on the brink of divorce, and wouldn't talk or make eye contact when in the studio. Tensions between the two reached a boiling point where Christine started dating the band's lighting director, resulting in the two having shouting matches. Mick discovered his wife was having an affair, which led to a divorce, and he and Stevie had a brief relationship.

To say emotions were running high is an understatement. Despite all the issues in the band, they channelled their heartbreak and anger into their music. Rumours was released on February 4, 1977 and became a phenomenal success. It won the Grammy for Album of the Year and became one of the best-selling albums of all time. In later years, Rumours was inducted into the Grammy Hall of Fame and was selected for preservation by the National Recording Registry.

The album was a success not only for the incredible instrumentation and vocal harmonies but the impeccable songwriting of Stevie, Lindsey, and Christine. Their emotions were expressed clearly in the songs with brutal honesty, as their lyrics were therapy sessions to process and move forward with their heartbreak. Lindsey's "Go Your Own Way" was his angry response to Stevie breaking up with him, whereas Stevie's "Dreams" was more positive. Other chart-topping songs from the album included "The Chain" and "Don't Stop," but only "Dreams" reached the number one spot.

However, as their fame rose, so did the critiques about whether they deserved it. Stevie got the worst, with constant sexist remarks about her place as a woman in rock music. She's insulted for her singing voice and for her lyrics about love and mysticism. During this time, Stevie also developed her signature style: long bohemian dresses, lace, corsets, and shawls, usually all in black. Coupled with the lyrics of her songs, many people started to believe she was an actual witch. The backlash Stevie received made her stop wearing black, and she chose more colourful clothes. But not long after, she reverted back to an all-black ensemble and told the public she's not a witch; she just preferred black clothing because it's slimming.

After Fleetwood Mac reached superstardom, they once again headed back into the studio for their next album. While their record label wanted them to record another Rumours-like record, the bank refused, deciding to take a more experimental approach. Tusk was released on October 12, 1979, and while it did perform well, it was deemed a failure to the record label for not reaching the same success as Rumours.

During the album's recording, tensions were still running high with the band, especially between Stevie and Lindsey. During this time, Stevie was in an on and off relationship with the Eagles lead singer, Don Henley, and had an unexpected pregnancy. Knowing a baby would put her career on hold, Stevie decided to have an abortion. The experience partly inspired her to write the song, "Sara," as if the child was a girl, Sara would have been her name. Along with "Sara," Stevie contributed four more songs to Tusk, but with such a back catalogue of songs in order for Christine and Lindsey to add their compositions, Stevie began to think of making a solo album.

Witchy Woman

Stevie released her first solo album, Bella Donna, on July 27, 1981. Her airy voice and heartfelt, mystical lyrics made the album a success, reaching number one on the Billboard 2oo list and going platinum in record sales. It's also during this album that she was able to showcase her witchy lyrics and style fully. The album produced the hits "Stop Draggin' My Heart Around" with Tom Petty and her signature song, "Edge of Seventeen."

Unfortunately, Stevie didn't get the chance to celebrate the release of Bella Donna. The night before the album's release, Stevie received a phone call from her best friend, Robin Snyder. Robin, who was pregnant, told Stevie she had leukaemia and was given three months to live. Robin's son, Matthew, was born three months early, and she died three days later. Utterly devastated, Stevie found comfort in her grief with Robin's husband, Kim Anderson. Out of their heartbreak and desire for Mathtthew's stability, the two married. Not long afterward, Stevie realized she had made a poor decision, and the two divorced.

Following those rollercoaster events, Stevie returned to Fleetwood Mac, releasing the Mirage album on June 18, 1982. The album performed well, with singles "Love in Store," "Hold Me," and "Gypsy," Stevie's tribute song to Robin.

Following the tour in support of Mirage, Stevie released her second solo album, The Wild Heart, on June 10, 1983, followed by Rock a Little in 1985. While touring for Rock a Little, Fleetwood Mac began recording their next album, Tango in the Night. While the album was a success and spawned hit singles, the recording process was a mess. Every member of the band except for John had their own solo projects, and since the success of Rumours, everyone was moving from one project to the next. Exhausted, the band's drug use grew exponentially, especially Stevie's. Her cocaine use became more of a means to get by than a want to get high. When the band went on tour to promote the album, unresolved issues in the band and constant fighting caused Lindsey to leave in the middle of the tour.

Following Lindsey's departure, Stevie visited a plastic surgeon in the hopes of getting a rhinoplasty. However, the appointment took a different turn, with the doctor telling Stevie her excessive cocaine use could kill her at any moment, and the amount that she was using has left her with a hole in her nose the size of a five-cent coin.

Panic-stricken, Stevie checked herself into the Betty Ford Centre for treatment and never touched cocaine again.

Leaving rehab, Stevie felt better than ever and was ready to take on the next phase in her life sober.

Stand Back

Adding two new members to the band, Fleetwood Mac released Behind the Mask on April 9, 1990. It performed modestly but with no hit singles. After going on tour, Stevie and Mick had an argument over the release of Stevie's song, "Silver Springs." The song, recorded during the making of Rumours, was discarded from the album after the band decided the album didn't need another ballad. Stevie wanted to include the song on her forthcoming album, but Mick knew the song was popular with fans and wanted to release it on an upcoming Fleetwood Mac box set, knowing it would be a selling feature. Not allowing her to use her own song, Stevie left the band.

After leaving Fleetwood Mac, the majority of the 90s were troubling for Stevie. In an attempt to ensure she wouldn't relapse into cocaine use; Stevie saw a therapist who prescribed her Klonopin. The intended results of the medication failed, and Stevie became dependent on it. Realizing the drug was changing her body mentally and physically, she headed for a detox program while her fifth solo album, Street Angel, was released on June 7, 1994.

Stevie hated the album, feeling that she didn't work hard enough in the production because of her Klonopin dependency. Furthermore, her record label rushed the final production of the album without Stevie's input, so by the time Stevie left her detox program, she could tour and promote the album.

Things finally turned around in 1997 when Stevie reunited with Lindsey, Mick, Christine, and John for The Dance. The live performance and album were a renewed success for the band, and they were inducted into the Rock and Roll Hall of Fame in 1998.

Feeling reinvigorated, Stevie and the rest of Fleetwood Mac, minus Christine, released Say You Will on April 15, 2003. The album peaked at number three on the charts and was the last album the band recorded.

Over the years, Stevie toured on and off with Fleetwood Mac and recorded two more albums, In Your Dreams in 2011 and 24 Karat Gold - Songs From the Vault in 2014.

She appeared in American Horror Story: Coven in 2014, playing a fictional version of herself as a witch, clearly playing into her aesthetic and getting the last laugh at critics who believed she's actually a witch. Her surprise appearance paid off as she returned in the eighth season.

In 2019, Stevie was inducted into the Rock and Roll Hall of Fame for a second time as a solo artist. She makes history with her accolade, as she's the first woman to be inducted twice.

Queen of Rock and Roll

Stevie has reached legendary status not only from the accolades she's received from her work but for her incredible talent. Her singing, songwriting, stage presence, and personality have made a lasting impact not only on rock and roll but the music industry as a whole.

A prime example came in 2020, when a Tik Tok video saw Nathan Apodaca riding a skateboard and drinking cranberry juice to the sound of "Dreams" went viral. The video resulted in a new wave of youth discovering Fleetwood Mac and Stevie's distinct vocals and songwriting capabilities. The song and album even returned to the charts, proving that the relatability in Stevie's lyrics about love and heartbreak are timeless.

Moreover, she's influenced and inspired so many women in music, including Beyonce, Sheryl Crow, Courtney Love, and Taylor Swift. Stevie has never been one to shy away from pouring her soul out into her lyrics. Her songs have been covered by many artists over the years, with each singer having their own connection to the lyrics. It's in the way she tied in mysticism and storytelling into her lyrics that made her songs captivating. Or in the way she performed with her ex-boyfriend for over 40 years, still bold enough to look him in the eyes and sing her songs about how much he meant to her. What can be more rock and roll than that?

Chapter 6: Madonna

The night is September 14, 1984, at Radio City Music Hall in New York City. What took place that night was a monumental moment in the music industry's history. It's the first-ever MTV Video Awards, a new and modern awards show highlighting the best music videos of the year.

The success of the show is crucial. MTV was at the top of its fame, being the go-to station for music news and entertainment. Thanks to MTV, the 80s was the golden age of music videos, as artists had a newer visual way to promote their songs. Music videos told a story of their own, adding clarity to the lyrics of a song, telling a different story altogether, showcasing the artist's aesthetic, and just showing fans what they look like. It was crucial to MTV that the awards show is a success and adds to the legacy they are building.

MTV executives reached out to a 26-year-old Madonna. A newcomer in the music industry whose fame was rapidly growing. She's also made her music videos in a style of her own, making her stand out against her peers, so it's no surprise when they asked her to open the show.

The show began with Madonna singing her hit single, "Like a Virgin." She was standing on top of a 17-foot-tall cake wearing a short, lacy wedding dress with a bustier top and a belt buckle reading 'boy toy.' As she made her way down the cake, she took off her veil and undid her updo, shaking her hair about. As she descended, one of her heels fell off. She rolled on the floor to cover the blunder as if it was planned and

55

stealthily put her heel back on. However, in the process of putting on her shoe, she accidentally flashed her underwear to the camera. She stood up and danced and twirled around on stage with her veil. Nearing the end of her performance, she dropped back down on the floor, the veil between her legs as she humps the air, before seductively lying down on the ground and rolling around once more with her dress over her head.

Once she left the stage, Madonna's management believed she had ended her career just as it was about to take off. But that was not the case.

The following morning, everyone was talking about Madonna's performance. From praise to controversy, Madonna was the stand-out from the entire show.

Her performance cemented her as a star and goes down in pop culture and MTV history.

It wouldn't be the first time Madonna made jaws drop, but it was the first moment leading up to her reign as the "Queen of Pop."

Who's That Girl

Madonna Louise Ciccone was born on August 16, 1958, in Bay City, Michigan, to parents Madonna Louise and Silvio Anthony 'Tony' Ciccone, becoming the first daughter out of six children. Madonna loved attention as a child, but with five siblings all needing their parents to notice them, Madonna learned she'd have to fight for what she wanted, so she would act out at any means necessary.

At 5 years old, her mother was diagnosed with breast cancer. Still too young to understand her mother's illness, Madonna would lash out at her, resulting in her mom being brought to tears. On December 1, 1963, her mom lost her battle with cancer.

Following her mother's death, she offered more support by helping her father out around the house. Fearful that someone would try to replace their mother, Madonna and her siblings would torment any housekeeper their father tried to hire, causing them to quit soon after. However, their plans failed, and in 1966, Tony married their housekeeper, Joan Gustafson, and the couple had two children together.

Still craving her father's recognition, Madonna put all her focus on schooling, being the only one out of her siblings getting high marks in all her classes. Still, her father didn't notice her the way she wanted, as her two older brothers were constantly getting in trouble for their bad behaviour.

Madonna decided to focus on getting attention in school for her unconventional behaviour. She still performed well academically but made a scene outside the classroom. During a talent show, she strutted around on stage, shimmied her hips and shoulders, and made flirtatious looks at the audience. At only 11 years old, her father was embarrassed, and the crowd was shocked.

Following the talent show, Madonna asked her dad to sign her up for jazz and tap dance lessons. She was a natural and went on to learn ballet. In 1976, she graduated from Rochester Adams High School and received a dance scholarship at the University of Michigan.

Being an overachiever, Madonna excelled in school and became an all-star in her class. During a weekend dinner with her family, Madonna told her father that the University of Michigan had taught her all she needed to know, and she was ready for the real world. She wanted to drop out and move to New York City and pursue a career in dance.

An argument between the two ensued, but Madonna held her ground, dropped out of school, and moved to the big city.

Centre Stage

19-year-old Madonna arrived in New York City in 1978. She couch surfed and auditioned for different dance companies before landing a position at the Pearl Lang Dance Theatre. She once again became a star student, performing Pearl's gruelling dance routines and practices; Pearl even cast her in one of her dance productions. However, Madonna's demeanour changed after she was held at knifepoint and forced to perform oral sex on a stranger. After a tough practice, during which Pearl ordered her to redo her dance nine times, Madonna stormed off the stage and never returned.

In May 1979, Madonna met musician Dan Gilroy. He began to teach her the guitar basics and how to write songs. She became obsessed, and just like everything else in her life, overachieved to be the best at songwriting and music. It worked, and Dan asked her to join his band, the Breakfast Club, as the drummer.

She didn't want to be hidden behind a big drum set, so she became the band's guitarist. She played the instrument well, and during live performances, she captured the audience's attention with her talent and stage antics. Eventually, Madonna grew tired of just being the guitar player and wanted to sing. She sang a few songs and believed the band could grow their fame if she became the lead singer. Dan said no, the two argued, and Madonna left the band.

Madonna decided to start her own band, reconnecting with her old boyfriend, Stephen Bray, forming the band, Emmy. During a performance,

Madonna invited music manager Camille Barbone to watch their show. Camille was impressed and wanted her to sign with her label, Gotham, on the condition she's a solo artist.

Express Yourself

Once she's signed as a solo act, Madonna dropped her last name from her performances and began to develop her signature 80s style, wearing thrift store clothes, rubber bracelets, bleach blonde hair, and ribbons to pull back her hair. Madonna started to record demos, but she and Camille clashed on the genre. Camille wanted Madonna to sing rock music, whereas Madonna wanted pop songs her fans could dance to. Realizing they were not on the same page, Madonna and Camille parted ways, and Madonna had to start all over again.

Madonna reached out again to Stephen and asked him to help her write songs and record demos. As DJs playing singles in clubs played a significant role in singers becoming famous, Madonna went to every club possible to grab a DJ's attention and have them play her demo. It worked, and one night she handed her demo to DJ Mark Kamins, and he played her song, "Everybody." Mark, who wanted to transition over to producing, tells Madonna he had connections at Sire Records. Mark planned a meeting between her and Seymour Stein, the label's president. Stein signed her for two singles before committing to an album. Of course, Madonna being Madonna, she put her all into the singles, bringing a high production value to "Everybody" and "Burning Up." Both singles topped the dance charts, and Sire Records, realizing Madonna's star power, signed her to record an album. She released her first album, Madonna, in 1983. The album was a hit, setting the standard for dance-pop, and had other female artists emulating her work throughout the 80s.

When the album is released, MTV is in the midst of becoming the go-to for music promotion. Madonna knew music videos would increase her fame and creativity and told Sire Records she not only wanted to make music videos but expensive ones. While she didn't get the exact budget she was looking for, she did get an increase for directors, sets, and wardrobes. Her music videos for "Everybody," "Burning Up, "Lucky Star," "Holiday," and "Borderline" set the bar high when it came to production and storytelling in music videos.

Madonna was ready to follow up with a second album, Like A Virgin. The first single, "Like A Virgin," was number one on Billboard for weeks. Its accompanying music video of Madonna dancing seductively on a boat in Venice and prancing around in a wedding gown promoted the song further with its heavy rotation on MTV.

It's also this point when Madonna's artistry and performances are critiqued. Conservative organizations called for a ban on her music due to her unabashed sexuality, clothing choices, and supreme confidence. Madonna paid no mind; she knew younger audiences look up to her as an inspiration, and for them to grow their confidence, sexuality was all that mattered to her.

Following her iconic MTV Video Awards performance, Like A Virgin was released on November 12, 1984, making Madonna an international star. She even became the first woman to sell five million copies of an album in the United States.

She released her second single, "Material Girl," and it was another success. But as much as Madonna loved the fame and fortune that her music had given her, she still wanted to do more. She decided the next career move for her should be an actress.

Starring Role

Madonna's big break into acting came in the 1985 film, Desperately Seeking Susan, a quintessentially 80s film about the interactions of two women living very different lives. The film was a box office hit and is even ranked as one of the best of 1985.

Madonna's next film was Shanghai Surprise in 1986, also starring her then-husband Sean Penn, in an attempt to save their deteriorating marriage. The movie was an absolute bomb, costing $17 million to make but only getting a return at the box office of $2.2 million.

While her marriage was spiralling out of control, Madonna still held the reins in her music, releasing True Blue in the same year. She co-wrote and co-produced the album, and unsurprisingly it was a hit. Seen as the album that made her the "Queen of Pop," True Blue showed Madonna's maturity and diversity in her songs. "Papa Don't Preach" tackled teen pregnancy, and the music video for "Open Your Heart" had Madonna playing a stripper, pushing the boundaries of sexual positivity over a female's body. The album even got a Guinness Book of World Records for the best-selling album by a woman.

In 1987 her film career was stagnant. She starred in Who's That Girl, and it's another failure, but the movie's soundtrack, in which she contributes four songs, was a commercial success. The album performing well compared to the movie indicates to Madonna that her career focus should definitely be on music, and soon enough, film offers dry up.

Not one to take no for an answer, Madonna decided it was time to go in a new direction, and she reinvented herself once more.

Like a Prayer

Madonna begins 1989 as a new woman. She dyed her blonde hair dark brown, changed her thrift store clothes to designer, and divorced Sean Penn. Madonna reflected on her marriage, Catholicism, her family, successes, and failures throughout this period, channelling them in her latest album, Like a Prayer.

Prior to the album's release, Pepsi reached out to Madonna for an endorsement deal, which was a huge promotional opportunity, as the only other artist who had an endorsement from a major company was Michael Jackson.

Madonna agreed and filmed an advertisement featuring the first single off her new album, "Like a Prayer." The following day, March 3, 1984, the "Like a Prayer" music video was released, and Madonna's level of controversy hit an all-time high.

The video featured burning crosses, her in a black slip dress with her straps falling off her shoulders, watching a group of white men kill a white woman, and a black man who finds her gets accused of a crime; she goes into a church where a statue of a Black Jesus comes to life, and they start kissing. The video is something no one has ever seen before, and Pepsi pulled their ad with Madonna, cancelling their partnership.

The music video didn't stop the sales of the album or her Blonde Ambition tour. If anything, it gave her more of the publicity she craved. On the tour, she debuted a high ponytail and coned bra corset. Her show was explicitly sexual, causing issues with religious groups and even governments.

But if people thought her concerts were too sexual, Madonna wanted them to know they hadn't seen anything yet.

A Little Risqué

The 1990s was a unique decade for Madonna. She starred in the film Dick Tracy, and similar to Who's That Girl, released I'm Breathless, a part-soundtrack, part-inspirational album for the movie. Her standout song, "Vogue," is on the album, resulting in the iconic Vogue dance and giving her her first hit of the decade.

She followed I'm Breathless with her first greatest hits album, The Immaculate Collection. It only featured two new songs with remixes and edits of her previous hits, but it became one of the best-selling greatest hits albums ever.

In 1991, she released the documentary Madonna: Truth or Dare, chronicling her Blonde Ambition tour. The film, just like her concert, was very sexual, but she gained praise for the normalization of homosexuality during a time when homophobia wasn't normalized. The film also solidified her place as an LGBTQ icon.

In 1992, she released Sex, the coffee table book that doubled as pornography and fetishism. It became a New York Times bestseller and the best-selling coffee table book ever. Alongside the book, she released Erotica, a concept album about sexuality. The album performed decently, but not to the standards Madonna was used to. Frankly, her fans and the media were tired of the overt sexuality from Sex and Erotica. Madonna just wanted people to liberate themselves sexually, but the public saw it as nothing more than constant shock value.

One positive event that occurs in 1992 is Madonna founded her own entertainment company, Maverick. The company's umbrella included a record label, film production, numerous publishing branches, and merchandising. Over the years, it had become the best artist-owned record label, signing innumerable artists who had gone on to have successful music careers.

In 1994, Madonna attempted to downplay her risqué image to a more sombre sound with 1994's Bedtime Stories but it was even less of a success than Erotica was.

Unsure of what to do next, Madonna looked back to acting. She had some success in a minor role in 1992's A League of Their Own, but she was still looking for her blockbuster film. Eventually, she heard of the musical Evita and realized that's her claim to fame for acting. Madonna related to Ava Perone, the Argentinian actress, politician, and activities by similar upbringings, opinions, and personality traits. However, due to being notoriously difficult to work with and her lack of success in film, no one in the movie's production wanted to hire her. But in typical Madonna fashion, no was not in her vocabulary. She wrote an impassioned four-page letter to the film's director, Alan Parker, proving she's the right fit for the role, and she'd be dedicated to filming.

Her letter worked, and she's cast. Madonna took the film seriously, taking singing and tango lessons. She put her heart and soul into the role, and it paid off. The film received mixed reviews, but Madonna was praised for her acting and won a Golden Globe for Best Actress in Motion Picture Musical or Comedy.

Hung Up

After the success of Evita, Madonna reinvented herself once more, this time with motherhood. Halfway through filming, Madonna discovered she was pregnant. After the birth of her daughter in 1996, her focus was on being a good mother and finding a new appreciation for spirituality and religion through the Jewish practice of Kabbalah. The result was the 1998 release of Ray of Light. The album brought her back to her pre-90s music success, containing pop, electronic, trance, and deeply personal lyrics. Ray of Light made history as the biggest sales for a female artist in its first week, and she won four Grammys.

Despite the album's success, critics began to comment on Madonna's age. Nearing 40, people within the music industry couldn't wrap their heads around a grown woman still making an impact on pop culture. Madonna was frustrated by the ageism but still pushed through, showing that her age does not affect her career.

She proved her point with the 2000 release, Music, a dance-pop electronica album with country references. Madonna reinvented her style once more, developing a cowgirl aesthetic for the album's era. The album was a critical success, along with the singles "Music" and "Don't Tell Me."

It's also during this time Madonna found love, this time in British director Guy Ritchie. The two got married on December 22, 2000 and had a son. During their relationship, Madonna adapted to British society, feeling more mature, elegant, and sophisticated.

With her lifestyle change into British society, Madonna reflected and compared how the Brits live and their culture with American life and culture, resulting in her ninth studio album, American Life.

Released on April 21, 2003, it was a concept album reflecting on everything in American society during that time. However, the album failed to get its message across, as she sang about moving away from the 'American Dream' and being materialistic, despite living said dream in England and having an iconic song entitled "Material Girl." The album also added commentary on America's war in Iraq, a very touchy subject for the country. The result is a less than stellar commercial and critical success for the album.

The Art of Reinvention

With new pop stars capturing the spotlight, Madonna refused to be pushed aside. So, on August 28, 2003, she returned to the MTV Video Music Awards stage, this time with Britney Spears and Christina Aguilera, the two biggest pop stars at the moment. The show began with a giant wedding cake, with Britney and Christina in almost identical wedding dresses from Madonna's 1984 performance. Nearly 20 years after the iconic performance, the two superstars performed "Like a Virgin," even rolling on the stage floor as she did.

Then, Madonna appeared at the top of the cake, dressed as the groom, and began singing her song, "Hollywood." She walked down the cake stairs to meet Britney and Christina. The three sang and danced before Madonna kissed Britney, followed by Christina. Once again, Madonna created a legendary MTV performance.

Madonna followed up the performance with the release of Confessions on a Dance Floor in 2005. The album was pure dance, letting inhibitions go and being free. The album was an absolute success, the first single, "Hung Up," hit number one in 41 countries and ties with Elvis Prestley as the artist with the most songs in top ten chart positions. Her concert in support of the album broke records for the highest-grossing concert for a woman. Over the years, she had made a revenue of $1.5 billion from concert tickets, making her the highest-grossing solo touring artist of all time.

In 2006, Madonna visited Malawi after she became aware of the country's extreme poverty and young children becoming orphaned due to their parents dying of AIDS. During her visit, she decided to establish the non-profit charity, Raising Malawi. The organization helped children with health care, with a no-charge intensive care unit and paediatric surgery ward. Another effort was education, building indoor schools so children didn't have to sit outside, along with making the schools closer to communities, so children didn't have to walk for miles, and a focus on educating girls. Lastly, the organization focused on community support, including help for orphan children, treatment centres for malaria and prevention, and a farm. While Madonna was in the process of setting up the charity, she and Guy adopted David Banda. In May 2009, Madonna adopted her second child from Malawi, Chifundo Mercy James as a single parent.

Madonna even found time to become an author, releasing five children's books that reached the New York Times bestseller list, and donated all the money from the books to a Los Angeles-based children's charity. She even found time to add fashion designer to her list. Collaborating with her daughter, Lourdes, she debuted the Material Girl clothing line in 2007, inspired by her iconic 80s fashion.

On March 10, 2008, Madonna was inducted into the Rock and Roll Hall of Fame. Soon after, she and

Guy divorced, and it inspired songs on her next album, 2008's Hard Candy, and went on the highly successful Sticky and Sweet tour.

Queen of Pop

Madonna released the albums MDNA in 2012, Rebel Heart in 2015, and Madame X in 2019. All being commercial and critical successes, redefining her style and sound for each album cycle.

Now at 63, Madonna still has no plans to slow down. During her awards speech for Billboard's Woman of the Year, Madonna got blunt and candid over the sexism and ageism she received throughout her entire career. Saying that even though she's been deemed controversial for her openness of sexuality, her only real controversy is sticking around for as long as she has.

Madonna's legacy is one of female empowerment and perseverance. Her refusal to be told no led her to become a fashion icon and change the sound of pop music. Along with her impact on music videos, she was the first female artist to capitalize on the potential of music videos, realizing the impact they could have on storytelling and promotion. Not only that, but she also influenced so many women in music to be explicit and comfortable in their sexuality and reinvent their sound and style throughout each album release.

Without Madonna flipping the music industry and pop culture on its head, who knows where the two would be? She's not named the "Queen of Pop" for nothing.

Chapter 7: Cher

It's 1996, and Cher was sitting down for an interview with Jane Pauley to promote her new album, It's a Man's World. The interview started off with Jane asking Cher questions about her life, career, and how she's maintained relevance for over three decades. Cher answered modestly, saying she always works hard and does whatever she wants.

But it's when Jane asked about the title of the album that things got interesting.

Cher explained that the album's name is tongue in cheek but also true. The world is run by men, and she's been dealing with their input for her entire career. She also said she feels bad for them. Toxic masculinity has a death grip on men, and they're not as strong compared to women in resilience and emotions.

Jane proceeded to ask Cher about her being quoted saying, "men aren't a necessity; they're a luxury." Cher still believed what she said, going into detail about how she viewed men as a 'dessert' and they're fun to have around, but she didn't need them to survive, and neither does every other woman. Jane looked shocked, but Cher continued with a story of a conversation she had with her mother. Cher said that her mother told her that she'll have to settle down and marry a rich man one day. Cher confidently responded, "Mom, I am a rich man."

This moment became an iconic quote for Cher, as it proved her toughness, independence, and power in a male-dominated industry.

And while men may be the dessert, Cher is the

main course.

Happy Was the Day We Met

On May 20, 1946, Cherilyn Sarkisian was born in El Centro, California, to Georgia Holt and John Sarkisian. Her parents divorced before Cher was even a year old, her mother remarried shortly after and had daughter Georganne, but that marriage ended in divorce as well, leaving Georgia a struggling single mother of two.

Georgia worked odd jobs while trying to get her career as a model and actress off the ground, and it was at 4 years old Cher realized she wanted to be a performer just like her mom. However, she didn't want to deal with the same career struggles her mom had. Try as she might, Georgia's career never took off, and she would struggle to make money, leaving the family dirt poor at certain points, dropping her daughters off at orphanages. Cher didn't start living full-time with her mother until she was three.

As she grew, Cher was more focused on seeing her name in lights than having good grades. She became rebellious, partying all night on the Sunset Strip, and her performance in school was less than stellar due to undiagnosed dyslexia. She dropped out of high school a year before graduating. While her mom was surprisingly supportive of her decision, the two argued over Cher being directionless in life and lying about her age to date older men.

Her rebellious streak continued, as after she dropped out, she moved out of her mom's house to live with her friend Melissa Melcher at just 16 years old. The girls got numerous receptionist and customer service jobs to pay their bills, but significant change was on its way for Cher. In November 1962, Cher met 27-year-old Sonny Bono while on a double date with

Melissa at a Hollywood restaurant. The two begin to date, and Cher quickly moved in with him after expressing she was no longer interested in her living arrangement after Melissa moved out.

Cher lucks out with meeting and dating Sonny, as he was a songwriter and assistant to record producer Phil Spector. Seeing this as an opportunity, Cher spent time at the recording studio with Sonny and contributed background vocals to "You've Lost That Lovin' Feelin'" by The Righteous Brothers, "Da Doo Ron Ron" by the Crystals, and "Be My Baby" by The Ronettes.

Sonny had his own aspirations to be a singer, but seeing the potential in Cher, he decided to focus on making her a star. He got Phil to produce a song for Cher called "Ringo I Love You." Recorded under the name Bonnie Jo Mason, the song was a flop, as listeners believed Cher's deep singing voice made her sound like a man, and therefore the song was about homosexuality.

After Cher's failure for a solo single, along with her constant stage fright, Cher and Sonny decide to try their luck at recording music together. They released three singles under the name Caesar and Cleo to zero fanfare. Nonetheless, they persisted and decided that going by their actual names could make a difference.

Introducing Sonny and Cher

The couple released their first big hit, "I Got You Babe," in 1965, reaching the number one spot on Billboard. Success came fast for the two, and people began to copy Cher's style. Her long shaggy black hair, bell bottoms, and ruffled shirts were everywhere.

As the two were growing in popularity, Sonny still wanted Cher to have her solo success and helped produce her first album, All I Really Wanna Do, at the end of 1965, with the album peaking in the top 20 charts.

The same year, Cher and Sonny also released their first album, Look at Us, reaching number two on Billboard. Along with "I Got You Babe," the album had four other hit songs on the charts, "The Beat Goes On," "Baby Don't Go," "A Cowboy's Work is Never Done," and "All I Ever Need is You" all in the top 20 charts, an accomplishment they only shared with Elvis Prestley and The Beatles.

Cher's solo career was also thriving, she released two albums in 1966, The Sonny Side of Cher and Cher, which were both huge successes.

However, things started to slowly come to a halt. America's social and political sphere changed in the late 60s to more rock and roll, and Sonny and Cher's upbeat pop songs didn't fit the culture. Along with being in a monogamous relationship, Sonny didn't want to follow the current music trends or lifestyle and their records as a duo, and Cher's solo work went into a free fall.

Sonny made a vanity project, the film Chasity starring Cher, in 1968, but it was a bomb. Sonny also began cheating on Cher repeatedly, but when he realized, he didn't want to lose her, they officially married (they had an unofficial marriage in a bathroom on October 27, 1964) following the birth of their child, Chaz Bono, on March 4, 1969.

By this time, the newlyweds were in crippling debt, and with a fraction of the fame they had, they performed at lounges and nightclubs. The two would have light-hearted banters on stage during their shows, which became the highlight of their shows. Realizing their potential, TV executives had them guest host on multiple primetime shows. Eventually,

Fred Silverman, the programming chief at CBS, saw them guest host on The Merv Griffin Show and decided they should have their own show.

The Sonny and Cher Comedy Hour premiered on August 1, 1971 and became a hit show for CBS ratings. Cher was praised for her comedic timing and deadpan humour, along with her clothes starting trends in 70s fashion.

It's also during the tenure of the show that Cher continued with her solo albums. Her single, 1971's "Gypsys, Tramps & Thieves," became her second number-one single, and the album of the same name was certified gold.

Cher's next two albums, Foxy Lady in 1972 and Half Breed in 1973, were chart-toppers, with the single "Half Breed" becoming her third number one song.

However, when things professionally were successful, behind the scenes, Cher's marriage wasn't. In 1972, Cher started to think of divorcing Sonny. They were both seeing other people while still living in the same house, albeit different corners, and kept up appearances for the show. Soon enough, the two reached a breaking point and cancelled The Sonny and Cher Comedy Hour in February 1974. Soon after the cancelation, Sonny filed for separation but Cher counters with filing for divorce. The proceeds get ugly as they battle over the custody of Chaz and their finances. While Cher won custody, Sonny took 95% of their income and made Cher pay him an extra $2 million. The reason behind the pay out to Sonny was due to Cher learning she was an employee of a company in her own name, Cher Enterprises, with Sonny as the president. Throughout all the work she created, Cher owned nothing.

On February 16, 1975, the first episode of Cher's variety show Cher aired and was a ratings hit. On top of honing her humour and skills from her show with Sonny, Cher's stage fright had completely disappeared. She dressed more scantily clad, with flowing, sheer, sequined dresses, crop tops, and just about anything that showed cleavage and skin.

Cher also finds love again, marrying Greg Allman of The Allman Brothers Band on July 30, 1975, days after her divorce from Sonny is finalized. The couple had a son, Elijah, on July 10, 1976, but they divorced in 1979.

Cher ended her variety show after one season and rebooted her show with Sonny. However, the magic that made the show a success is gone, and it got cancelled after two seasons.

With her albums failing, Cher headed to Las Vegas for a revamp, not even beginning to realize what the 80s were about to offer her.

Starting Over

Cher released the disco-inspired hit "Take Me Home" and the album of the same name in 1979, both became her first musical successes in five years. However, the success didn't last long, she finally released the rock album she's been passionate to make for years, Prisoner, in the same year, and it was a failure.

During this time, she was performing her residency at Caesars Palace in Las Vegas, and while the residency was a financial triumph, Cher was still feeling the need to scratch her life-long-acting itch. She cancelled her residency and headed to Hollywood. Upon arrival, no one in Hollywood would give her the time of day, so once again, she packed up and moved with her kids to New York City and landed a role in the Broadway play, Come Back to the 5 and Dime, Jimmy Dean, Jimmy Dean. During a performance, director Mike Nichols was impressed with her acting and offered her a role in his upcoming movie, Silkwood, alongside Meryl Streep.

Silkwood premiered in 1983, and when Cher is listed as a cast member, the public questions her acting ability. On one occasion, Cher remembered going to a theatre, and upon seeing the trailer, the audience laughed when her name was shown. However, Cher came out on top, receiving an Oscar nomination for Best Supporting Actress and won a Golden Globe for Best Supporting Actress.

In 1985, she had a leading role in Mask. She played a biker with a drug and alcohol addiction who tries to raise her son, who has craniodiaphyseal dysplasia. The film was another critical and box office success.

Now that Hollywood finally took Cher seriously, the offers for roles kept coming in. In 1987, she starred in three movies: Suspect, The Witches of Eastwick, and Moonstruck. All the films were hits, but Moonstruck, in particular, garnered Cher the most accolades. At 42, she won an Academy Award for Best Actress and the Golden Globe for Best Actress - Motion Picture Comedy or Musical.

As her acting career was an ultimate triumph, the media went crazy over her personal life. She dated Gene Simmons of KISS and actor Val Kilmer and got criticized for dating men much younger than her. She went on to tell the media that men her age and older are intimidated by her, whereas younger men are not, along with the hypocrisy that if the genders were reversed, the tabloids and media wouldn't care.

Seriously Rockin'

In 1987, Cher took another try at rock music with her self-titled album, Cher. This time, the album was a triumph, with her rock ballad, "I Found Someone," being her first number-one single in years. The new album coincides with a new look for her album era. She admitted to fixing her teeth, getting plastic surgery on her breasts and nose, and began wearing provocative, lacy black clothes, specifically thong bodysuits.

Cher carried this fashion look in the promotion of Heart of Stone in 1989. The album's smash hit, "If I Could Turn Back Time," received controversy for its music video. The video saw Cher performing on the USS Missouri, straddling a cannon and dancing around in a bodysuit on top of a fishnet body stocking, leaving her buttocks exposed, resulting in MTV only playing the video after 9:00 p.m.

In 1990, Cher starred in Mermaids, a film that was relatively similar to her upbringing. She played a carefree mother who moved around the country with her two young daughters after every breakup. It was once again a critical and commercial success.

She released Love Hurts in 1991 and accompanied the album with a tour. However, things don't go as planned. Halfway through the tour, she contracted Epstein-Barr virus and suffered from chronic fatigue as a result, leaving her unable to continue music and films. Cher eventually recovered and released It's a Man's World in 1995. While the album doesn't perform well in the United States, it reaches number 10 on the UK charts.

Utter heartbreak struck Cher on January 5, 1998, when Sonny died from injuries after hitting a tree on a skiing trip. Sonny's wife asked Cher to give his eulogy, and she delivered a heart-breaking goodbye to her former lover and collaborator.

The same year, she released Believe. The lead single of the same name was a chart-topper, and Cher was the first artist to use Auto-Tune for the song. "Believe" went on to be one of Cher's most recognizable songs, and the dance-pop album won her a Grammy for Best Dance Recording.

The Music's No Good Without You

In 2001, Cher released Living Proof and, while going on tour for the album, announced she'd be retiring from live shows, and this tour would be her farewell. The farewell tour was an incredible achievement. She kept extending the concert, but it grossed over $145 million when her final show came, making her the most successful female touring artist ever.

However, her retirement didn't last long as she went on tour in 2014 and 2019. She starred in the musical Burlesque in 2010, which was a box office hit. Cher makes an appearance in the film Mama Mia! Here We Go Again and released an album of Abba covers.

Cher was also seen as a gay icon. Her role as a lesbian in Silkwood initially led the way for her praise in the LGBTQ community, and over the years, her ever-changing, eccentric style influenced the gay community, specifically drag queens. Moreover, her child, Chaz, is transgender. Cher revealed when Chaz came out, she wasn't happy or accepting, but after 24 hours, Cher realized how stupid she was acting and embraced her child with open arms, further leading her to accepting and advocating LGBTQ rights.

Currently, Cher spends her time on philanthropic and political efforts; she made headlines in 2020 for traveling to Pakistan and moving the world's loneliest elephant to a sanctuary in Cambodia. She also established the CherCares Pandemic Resource and Response initiative following the COVID-19 pandemic. In partnership with the head doctor of the Pandemic Resource and Response Centre at Columbia University, she donated over $1 million to areas in America where citizens are neglected and in need of health services.

Cher's legacy is one of a diva who never backs down and keeps adapting as the years and decades change, finding a way to be part of pop culture without conforming to its standards. She never listened to the haters, never catered to a man, and never does anything she doesn't want to. She's made a lasting impression on the music and film industry, pop culture, and fashion. At 75, there's still so much she can accomplish.

At this point, it's definitely not a man's world. It's Cher's world.

Chapter 8: Bjork

When someone is asked about Bjork, they'll most likely associate her with her iconic swan dress from the 2001 Academy Awards. Then they'll remember her as a musician. It's interesting that after a career spanning over four decades, multiple albums hitting the Billboard 200 chart, and selling millions of records, she's still most recognized for wearing an unusual dress.

Maybe it's because her music is unique from what a majority of society is listening to. Her music was considered atmospheric, an experience, albums that you don't listen to just for easy listening; you have to pay attention. The consensus around Bjork was that her music isn't for everyone, and if one is a fan, they have a more refined, elitist taste in music.

But Bjork disagreed, she's claimed many times her music is pop and is for everyone, and with every album focusing on different production techniques, genres and styles, there probably is a Bjork song out there for everyone to enjoy. Not only that; she's been ahead of her time with adding technology into her music, something she doesn't get the credit she deserves.

Therefore, it's time to change the narrative about Bjork.

One Day

Bjork Guomundsdottir was born on November 21, 1965, in Reykjavik, Iceland. Her mother, Hildur Runa Hauksdottir, and father, Guomundur Gunnarsson, were polar opposites in lifestyles and ideals. Her mother was more rebellious and free-spirited, while her father was more practical and hardworking. Their differences led to them divorcing when Bjork was two years old.

She lived with her father and immediately showed she had an ear and talent for music. Bjork put on impromptu performances for family and friends. At five years old, her parents enrolled her in the Icelandic Conservatory of Music. Even at such a young age, Bjork was independent. She was introverted, only having a handful of friends who were outcasts like her, but preferred spending time alone and thinking of music. She listened and became interested in classic and avant-garde artists with a dash of pop.

Her stepfather, Saevar Arnasson, was a musician and helped grow her love of music, eventually encouraging her to perform in a school recital. She performed "I Love to Love" by Tina Charles. Her performance was so impressive, teachers sent off a song recording to the local radio station. Bjork's performance was played on heavy rotation, resulting in the song becoming popular and Bjork becoming a local celebrity. The song led to Saevar securing a record deal with Falkinn Records. Bjork released her first self-titled album at the age of 11 in 1977.

Punk Girl

Bjork was asked to record a second album but refused. She didn't want to record cover songs; she wanted to record her own. So, instead, she focused on being a child and, in her teens, discovered punk music.

She started joining punk bands at the age of 14. The first of many is the all-girl punk band, Spit and Snot, as the drummer before joining a new-wave band, Exodus. Formed with other school members, they were overachievers with intense song arrangements. They released a cassette and made an appearance on a local TV show but disbanded soon after.

Shortly after the disbanding of Exodus, Bjork joined another band, Jam80, originally performing disco covers. Later they rebranded, changing their name to Tappi Tikarrass and creating their own music. Bjork left the band to form a different one, Kukl, eventually becoming The Sugarcubes.

The Sugarcubes gave Bjork her first taste of success and her first child. While in the process of forming The Sugarcubes, Bjork married the band's guitarist, Por Eldon, and they had a son, Sindri Eldon Porsson, on June 8, 1986. However, their marriage didn't last long, and they divorced the same year their song was born.

The Sugarcubes' first album, Life's Too Good, was released in 1989 and became an underground success in the U.S. and UK with a cult-like fanbase due to their hit song, "Birthday." Moreover, The Sugarcubes became the most successful rock band to come out of Iceland. But Bjork had other plans; in between successful North American and European tours for their next three albums, Bjork started focusing on solo work. She left the band, resulting in their breakup, following their final tour stop in Reykjavik for their last album, Stick Around for Joy, in 1992.

Now on her own for the first time since her debut album at 11 years old, Bjork moved to London to begin the next stage of her solo career.

Hunter

When Bjork moved to London, she began working on her debut album alongside producer Nellee Hooper, titled Debut. Released on July 5, 1993, the album was a blend of genres that Bjork had a current interest in. Songs on Debut featured the genres of jazz, pop, electronica, and trip-hop. While it was a wild blend of genres, the album worked; Bjork was recognized for bringing house music to the mainstream, and the album sold over half a million copies.

Released during the grunge era of music, Bjork stood out with her gliding voice and her songwriting of love and youthful wonder. Moreover, the world wasn't used to hearing or seeing someone like her. Her appearance and voice made the media see her as a cute child, an elf, or a pixie. She was a stranger from a strange land with a unique personality and style; she didn't fit the Icelandic stereotype, so the North American media came up with their own.

After the release of Debut, Bjork upped her technology game. Realizing the potential of technology and the internet, she launched her website in 1994. In an attempt to see how far the capabilities of the internet can go, she attempted live streaming when dial-up was still the main way to access the internet.

Bjork followed the success of Debut with Post on June 13, 1995. The album was a sky-rocket success, blending the sounds of dance, techno, and art-pop but with an edge. Whereas her first album was about taking in the beauty of what's around her since moving to London, Post had her going out and living in the city. Bjork also lined up artful music videos to the album's six singles, all of which were praised for their unique visuals. Over the years, the uniqueness and creativity of Post led it to be included in numerous 'best of' album lists.

The triumph of Post led to the media wanting to know more about Bjork. However, deciding she wanted to focus on music instead of being a celebrity, she became notoriously private; she didn't get into many details of her personal life after the release of Debut. So, the media and paparazzi tried to dig for information themselves by bothering her friends and family. Things reach a breaking point when at a Bangkok airport. She attacked a reporter after harassing her and her son. No charges were pressed, and Bjork apologized to the reporter, but she got her point across that she wanted to be left alone.

Her third album, Homogenic, was released on September 22, 1997, which is when Bjork fully embraced experimental art-pop and electronic music. Homogenic was a concept album about Iceland. During the writing process, Bjork began to question who she was as an international star and if she still felt Icelandic. She wanted her songs to be Icelandic pop with the instrumentation reflecting the sounds and experiences of Iceland. For the album's first single, "Joga," Bjork went to a volcano in Iceland and recorded the bubbles from the holes in a volcano and edited them into a beat. Her homage to Iceland worked, as it reached number one in her native country and reached the top 20 charts on Billboard.

I've Seen it All

In 2000, Bjork was asked to star in Lars von Trier's musical Dancer in the Dark. She played the starring role as a Czech immigrant factory worker in the United States who, while going blind, tried to save money to afford a surgery that would prevent the same degenerative disease for her son. Bjork's acting was praised as she won and received nominations for her acting. She also produced, wrote, and sang for the soundtrack along with its Academy Award-nominated song, "I've Seen it All." She performed the song at the Oscars wearing the infamous swan dress.

In 2001, she released Vespertine, a much slower record than her last three. Bjork focused on micro beats and once again turned to technology to create the beats she wanted, even focusing on how the sound would be with digital downloads. Bjork called the album 'introverted' in regard to her senses, sexuality, and mentality. Of course, Bjork puts a lot of effort into the album's visual component with her music videos. However, the videos contained sexual acts and nudity, resulting in little to no airplay on MTV.

This was also a significant moment in her life, as she moved from London to New York during the making of Vespertine. After she moved, she met artist Matthew Barney and the two started a relationship and had a daughter, Isadora, in 2002.

Medulla was released in 2004, and once again, Bjork took a completely different approach to the album's creation. Save for some tech developments, a few instruments, and backing sounds made by humans, the album was entirely a cappella. The album positions highly on the US and UK charts. She even received Grammy nominations for Best Female Pop Vocal Performance and Best Alternative Music Album.

Her next release in 2007, Volta, became the first album to reach the top 10 on the Billboard 200. The African-inspired album featured her collaborating with well-known producer Timbaland and focused on topics of community and finding one's primal side. Shortly after the release, she went on the Volta Tour, a high-tech tour featuring electronic instruments, like the Reactable to create different sounds and beats on a lit-up table, and the Tenori-on, a system that turns light into sound patterns.

She released her next concept album, Biophilia, on October 5, 2011. Biophilia covered issues in Iceland over the 2008-2011 financial crisis along with the impact of technology and nature. The album was quite literally electronic, as most of it was created on an iPad. Staying true to the technological impact of the album, each song had a corresponding app to download that teaches about music, the first album ever to do so.

With the release of Vulnicura in 2015, Bjork ended her long-term relationship with Matthew. The album focused on their breakup and Bjork's heartbreak. "History of Touches" talked about her attempts to keep her family together, rejection, and the breaking of promises. Whereas the final song on the album, "Quicksand," had her coming to terms with her relationship's end. Vulnicura was highly successful, even deemed one of Bjork's best albums.

Bjork once again included technology in her album, this time with virtual reality. The music video for "Stonemilker" was done with 360 cameras. Bjork used drones and 3D printing to create the Bjork Digital exhibition at different venues worldwide.

Her latest album, Utopia, was released on November 24, 2017, to critical acclaim. The album was the opposite of Vulnicura. When she toured for the previous album, the audience was sad along with her, mourning their own end of relationships, and Bjork realized she didn't want to make that kind of album again. Filled with flutes and real-life bird calls, the album was hopeful. The album was once again nominated for the Best Alternative Music Album at the Grammys for the eighth year in a row.

All is Full of Love

With a career spanning over 30 years, Bjork is more than all the umbrella terms for someone in the music industry; she's a true artist. While most music listeners may brush her off for being 'weird,' it's mainly because they won't take the time to listen to what she has to say.

Bjork is a storyteller, and each song and album revolves around specific events and experiences that are easy to comprehend when listening with an open mind.

Bjork stands out from her peers for being a pioneer in adding technology to her music before the rest of the industry caught on to help, adapt, and change the way music is made. She's also an artist that focuses on every detail of an album release. From the characters she created on the album covers so they're a visual representation of what her fans can expect to listen to, and her music videos catering to the sound and content of her songs, she took the concept of how to market an album and made it her own.

However, she rarely gets the proper recognition she deserves because of being surrounded by men. She had to fight to be the one in control of producing her albums, and while she's collaborated with multiple producers (who are mostly men), they're the ones getting the credit regardless of how many songs they contributed to.

With a majority of her albums reaching the top 20 slots on the Billboard 200, multiple Grammy nominations, and selling millions of records, Bjork's achievements are hers and hers alone. She's so much more than that swan dress.

Chapter 9: Beyonce

It's April 23, 2016, and Beyonce shocked her fans by dropping a new album, Lemonade. She accompanied the album with a film of the same name, and once they're both released, fans jumped at the opportunity to listen and see what Beyonce's new album is all about.

They were in for a surprise.

The album was broken into several chapters. The songs touched on many important topics in Beyonce's life, but the main storyline of the album is the revelation that her husband, Jay-Z, had an affair. The album went through the seven stages of grief while weaving the systemic problems Black women face in America.

With songs like "Hold Up" and "Sorry," Beyonce didn't hold back. She was angry, she was heartbroken, and she was laying it all out on the table. "Daddy Lessons" compared Jay-Z's infidelity to her father cheating on her mother. While the final song "Formation" had Beyonce growing from the affair, bonding with the women in her life so she, and all other women who have dealt with trauma, can rise up, change, and move forward.

The album was unique, introspective, illustrative, and relatable. It catapulted to the top of the charts, with fans angry at Jay-Z's infidelity and wanting to know who the mistress is.

Beyonce also brought the generational trauma of Black women to the masses, telling the world this cycle needs to break and that the Black men in their lives need to be better.

The album received multiple Grammy awards along with other accolades. Beyonce proved she's a force to be reckoned with. She made a concept album popular again during a time of streaming and singles; she turned songs into anthems and lyrics into quotes. She had the world wanting to know who Becky was.

Lemonade proved that Beyonce doesn't take part in the music industry. She changes it.

Me, Myself, and I

Beyonce Giselle Knowles was born on September 4, 1981, in Houston, Texas, to parents Tina and Michael. Along with her younger sister, Solange, the family lived an upper middle-class lifestyle. Tina owned a hair salon, and Matthew is a salesman.

During her childhood, Beyonce was bullied for her name and appearance, and she withdrew and became very shy as a result. However, Tina noticed that when Beyonce sings, she lit up and became her past self before the bullying. Thinking performing would give her daughter her confidence back, Tina enrolled Beyonce in dance classes, and Beyonce opened up; she was a natural performer.

One day, after one of her dance classes, her teacher, Darlette Johnson, was humming the tune of a song. Beyonce, who was waiting for her parents to pick her up, recognized it and sang the song perfectly. Darlette is shocked at Beyonce's talent and, with the permission of Tina and Michael, had her perform at a local talent show. Darlette also connected with one of her friends, Debra and Denise, who had been traveling around Houston to find young girls to form a singing group.

At just eight years old, Debra and Denise could not believe the raw talent and stage presence Beyonce had, and they asked her to formally audition for the group. She made it and joined the group, Girls Tyme. Beyonce befriended two other members of the group, Kelly Rowland and LaTavia Roberson, and the girls were constantly over at Beyonce's house, practicing their singing and dancing.

During this time, Matthew saw the potential in the girls to really make it big in the music industry, and he took their practices to the next level. In one instance, he had the girls run for miles while singing so they could learn breath control when they perform. Girls Tyme even appeared on Star Search, performing an original song, but they didn't win. Eventually, Matthew decided that the only way the girls will succeed is if he's the one managing them. He quit his job to manage them full time, hired professionals to help with their voices and dance, and cut the group members from six to four.

In 1995, Matthew sent a tape of the group to a talent scout at Columbia Records. The scout was intrigued and had the girls perform a showcase for her, and they were signed.

Destiny's Child

The group rebranded once more, this time with their name. They went from Girls Tyme to Destiny's Child and released their self-titled album in 1998. It was a moderate success, but their follow up, "The Writing's on the Wall," gave them their breakthrough success with singles "Jumpin' Jumpin'," "Bills, Bills, Bills," and "Say My Name." With the latter winning two Grammy awards.

However, tensions in the group were rising. LaTavia and LeToya Luckett expressed their frustrations with Michael being the group's manager, and him always positioning Beyonce as the leader of the group. The girls wanted him out. However, the reverse happened, and the two were replaced with Michelle Williams and Farrah Franklin. Although not long after Farrah joined, she left, leaving Destiny's Child a trio.

Beyonce began to stand out in the group and was offered an acting role as the lead in the TV movie Carmen: A Hip-Hopera in 2001. Her acting debut coincided with the release of Destiny's Child's third album, Survivor, which sold over 10 million copies and featured hits "Bootylicious" and "Survivor." The trio gained more recognition from their unique style, ripped clothes, colourful, unique patterns, and crop tops. All thanks to Beyonce's mom for designing them.

It's not only Destiny's Child's fashion sense, but their songs standing out during a very bubble gum pop era.

In 2002, Beyonce made her second film and theatrical debut in Austin Powers in Goldmember. The movie hit number one on the weekend box office following its release. Afterward, Destiny's Child announced their hiatus so everyone could focus on their solo work.

Going Solo

Beyonce met her future husband, Jay-Z, when they duetted on the song "03 Bonnie & Clyde" and the single reached number four on the Billboard charts. Soon afterward, Beyonce released her first solo album, Dangerously in Love, on June 23, 2003, and featured one of Beyonce's signature songs "Crazy in Love" featuring Jay-Z. The album sold over 11 million copies and went on to win five Grammy awards.

In 2004, following the success of her first album, Destiny's Child reunited for their final album, Destiny Fulfilled, and it peaked at number two on Billboard.

Over the years, the group's albums have sold over 60 million copies. They are known as one of the most famous and successful girl groups.

Now completely solo, Beyonce had the media, fans, and music in the palm of her hand.

Irreplaceable

Beyonce released her second album, B'Day, on September 4, 2006—her 25th birthday. The album was recorded in three weeks and was another massive success for the singer, featuring another one of her signature songs, "Irreplaceable." The album was nominated for another five Grammys and won the award for Best Contemporary R&B album. The album was so popular that it got re-released a year later with five more songs and went on again to be nominated for two Grammys.

While promoting B'Day, the two movies, The Pink Panther and Dreamgirls, were released. She starred alongside Steve Martin for The Pink Panther, and the comedy hit big at the box office. Dreamgirls was an adaptation of the Broadway musical with Beyonce as the lead. Critics and Beyonce believed the film was going to be her acclaimed starring role, however, her co-star Jennifer Hudson stole the show, and the media tried to pit the two women against each other in a feud, which Beyonce shut down. The film performed tremendously at the box office, but critics said Beyonce's performance fell short while Jennifer received critical fame and won the Oscar for Best Supporting Actress. To add insult to injury, Beyonce's song, "Listen" for the movie's soundtrack, was nominated for Best Original Song; however, only three songwriters could be credited, and Beyonce is left off the nomination. The decision sparked old rumours that Beyonce didn't write or barely wrote her own songs but still took credit for them.

Beyonce tried to push the critics off and embarked on her The Beyonce Experience world tour and got married to Jay-Z on April 4, 2008.

She's Fierce

Beyonce released I Am...Sasha Fierce on November 12, 2008. It was a concept album of sorts. One night while on tour, Beyonce got absolutely lost in her performance. She realized this boldness, sexiness, and pure fierceness she exhibited on stage and called her Sasha Fierce, her alter ego. Offstage, she's shy and private, so Beyonce decided to tie her two personalities together for the double album.

The I Am side contains pop and R&B songs. She would release two ballads from this side of the album, "If I Were a Boy" and "Halo," which performed well in the charts.

The Sasha Fierce side was upbeat pop, electronic, and hip-hop tracks. She released more singles from Sasha Fierce than I Am, but it was the mega-showstopper, "Single Ladies (Put a Ring on it)," that blew the album up. However, "Single Ladies" also causes a controversial moment in pop culture history. At the 2009 MTV Video Music Awards, the single was nominated for Best Video by a Female Artist. While many would have thought Beyonce would win, it was Taylor Swift for her song, "You Belong With Me," that won. As Taylor started her acceptance speech, Kanye West stormed on stage, stole the mic from her, and announced, "Beyonce had one of the best videos of all time." He passed the mic back to Taylor, who had tears in her eyes and was at an utter loss for words. Beyonce was shocked and embarrassed by Kanye's actions. Later on in the show, Beyonce won for Video of the Year; she gave up her speech so Taylor could finish hers and have her moment. Beyonce was praised for her olive branch to Taylor, considering she was collateral damage to Kanye's outburst. The moment went down in pop culture and the award show's history; the following day, it was deemed the unfortunate highlight of the show, with everyone talking about it, including President Obama.

"Single Ladies (Put a Ring on it)" hit number one on Billboard, became another one of her standout songs, and even started a dance craze thanks to the music video. She received seven Grammy nominations and won a record-setting six.

In 2009, Beyonce went on tour in support of the album, and when the tour's promoter, Live Nation, checked the finances for the tour, they realized funds were missing. The culprit turned out to be her father. Shocked, Beyonce confronted her father. While her father was still her manager, things were rocky between the two. Beyonce started her own management company, resulting in her father losing money from her, and he was having multiple affairs. When the allegations were proven true, she made the decision to fire her father as her manager.

Run the World (Girls)

After taking a brief hiatus, Beyonce released 4 on June 24, 2011. The album was her first venture into different sounds that weren't classic pop or R&B sounding; she mixed rock and Afrobeat on her songs. The album was another success, giving her her fourth consecutive number one album. She also headlined the Glastonbury Festival at the Pyramid Stage, being the first woman-let alone Black woman- to headline the festival in 20 years. (Funnily enough, Jay-Z was the first rapper to headline the festival in 2008).

Following this monumental event, Beyonce performed her single "Love on Top" at the 2011 MTV Video Music Awards. After she performed, she unbuttoned her blazer and rubbed her belly, announcing she's pregnant. She and Jay-Z's daughter, Blue Ivy Carter, was born on January 7, 2012.

Following the birth of their daughter, Beyonce went on two different tours with Jay-Z to skyrocketing success, becoming one of the most successful tours of all time. Then, she released Beyonce on December 13, 2013. Her single, "Drunk in Love," featuring her husband, was a huge success, and the album unsurprisingly tops the charts and wins Beyonce Grammys.

2014 saw Beyonce expand her business ventures in athletic wear. She partnered with Top Shop to create Ivy Park, named after her daughter, and the parks she would go for runs in when she was a child. The athleisure clothing of sports bras, leggings, sweatsuits, and t-shirts was praised for its style and comfort. In 2018, she bought out the 50% Top Shop owner Philip Green had in the company after sexual assault allegations were brought against him, now having 100% ownership of her brand.

Beyonce played the Super Bowl Halftime Show on February 7, 2016, to rave reviews; she even reunited with Michelle and Kelly to perform their Destiny's Child's hits "Bootylicious" and "Independent Women Part I." Then released Lemonade on April 23, 2017. The album was arguable her best to date; she was open and raw about Jay-Z's affair, the state of her marriage, her Black heritage and upbringing, police brutality, and slavery. Jay-Z received a lot of criticism for his infidelity, even issuing a public apology, but the album also received praise and started a conversation around the history and lives of Black people in

America. The album won a Peabody Award and multiple Grammys.

While riding on the success, Beyonce announced she's pregnant with twins Rumi and Sir, who were born on June 13, 2017.

A year later, in a fully stable marriage, Beyonce and Jay-Z went on tour together again, the On the Run II tour, grossing over $250 million. While finishing their second London show, Beyonce told the audience she and Jay-Z had a surprise for them. The music video for "Apeshit" started playing. It's a duet by Jay-Z and Beyonce singing about their success and lifestyle. The music video was visually appealing, as the two rented out the Louvre, having historical artwork as their backdrop. When the music video finished, a title card announced, 'album out now.' Everything is Love, released with the artist's name The Carters, was another hit album for Beyonce and received positive reviews.

Since the incredible success of Lemonade, Beyonce lent her voice to the 2019 The Lion King remake and released Black is King, a companion visual album to the film, which received six Grammy nominations and won two. Those nominations, coupled with her other wins and nominations throughout her entire career, made her the most awarded female and singer in Grammys history.

Queen B

At the time of writing this book in 2021, Beyonce will turn 40 years old. With not even half a century alive, Beyonce's career is one of talent, determination, and a work ethic revolving around never saying no to what you truly want.

Her music resonates with high production value, who she chooses to collaborate with, and what she wants to sing and write about. Her fans can put on "7/11," her song about partying and letting loose, while they too are planning to go out for a couple of drinks. Then there's "Freedom," a song about power and resilience, which can be reflective during a time of racial injustice.

Her success isn't just based on the number of awards, nominations, and achievements, but on how she's impacted pop culture at large. She is loved by fans all over the world, regardless of age, gender, or race. She's a Black woman who dominates and takes up space in every aspect of her career, which influences so many artists, her mesmerizing stage presence, choreography, and vocal capabilities, her fashion choices, and bringing Black culture to mainstream recognition.

She hasn't just changed pop culture; she is the culture.

In an interview during the promotion of B'Day, an interviewer asked her what she would like to be known for. Beyonce replied, "a legend in the making." Well, she's not 'in the making' anymore.

Conclusion

All the singer-songwriters in this book have impacted the music industry and pop culture in some shape or form. Their stories are included, not only to describe their accomplishments, but to touch on the broader subject of what women have to do to turn their dreams of becoming an artist into reality.

As I mentioned at the beginning of the book, it may seem that a woman's career in any department of the music industry in 2021 is higher than ever, especially if you think back to when Carole King, Cher, and Dolly Parton were starting out. Still, statistically, there's been little improvement.

Below are the significant factors that the artists in this book, and those in the industry today, deal with as setbacks to their artistry

Reinvention

Artists like Beyonce, Madonna, and Cher all had to reinvent themselves at some point during their careers. Trying new sounds, genres, and fashion trends are not the problem; we all change and evolve over time. The problem lies with the men who perform in the same genres as these women when they get famous. They can continue releasing the same sound and genre of music for their entire career without issue. Whereas for female artists to stay relevant and continue to make the music they want, they're under constant transformation.

Production

Production is one of the most continuous male-dominated fields in the music industry. Women can barely catch a break in this boy's club, but even when they do, they're still not recognized. Unless one is a dedicated Bjork fan, not many people know the level of production she does when creating her albums. She's mentioned in past interviews that she wished she took pictures of herself in the studio so people would believe her when she said she's a producer. Even in the release of her work, the media will constantly focus on who she collaborates with, the men getting all of the credit.

Bjork isn't the only one. Beyonce and Madonna spent a lot of time on their sound and vision for their albums, but since a majority of the producers they worked alongside are men, they receive the credit.

Songwriting

Every single woman in this book has written their own songs, but unless they're the only songwriters, their acknowledgments for their skills at writing lyrics were low. Moreover, when a female singer writes alongside another songwriter or sings a song from someone else's catalogue, it's usually a man. For instance, in 2020, the UK signing rights organization PRS for Music had a 60% increase in female songwriters, but they were still significantly outnumbered by male songwriters. Additionally, PRS for Music states that female songwriters face incredible hurdles to achieve success compared to their male counterparts, with the top 10 female songwriters generating 67% less revenue from royalties than the top 10 men.

Ageism

Dolly Parton, Cher, and Madonna have all been told at some point they're at the 'phasing out' stage in their careers due to their age. They've been told that they're too old to wear fashionable clothes or release new music and should therefore retire. Thankfully, the three of them never listened. Yet it's very telling of the beauty standards placed on women in the music industry, especially if you consider there are some men who rose to fame at the same age as Dolly, Cher, and Madonna, and they are still making music without the critiques of their appearance or when they'll retire.

Awards and Achievements

Despite all these women receiving awards and achievements for their music, major accolades are still predominantly given to men. The Grammys are mentioned consistently throughout this book, with almost every single artist receiving one. In the Annenberg Inclusion Initiative, their report indicated that in the five biggest categories (Record of the Year, Album of the Year, Song of the Year, Best New Artist, and Producer of the Year), female nominees have risen over the years, with 21.8% in 2021. But from 2013 to 2021, the average is 13.4% women versus 86.6% of men. If you think about it, it does make sense. Bjork is constantly nominated in album categories but has yet to win, and while Beyonce had set a world record for the amount of Grammy wins she has, she's been nominated for more of her work than she's won.

Women of Colour

The business side of the music industry that is held behind closed doors doesn't add much improvement for women of colour either. Figures have shown that from 2012 to 2020, women consist of 21.6% of artists, 12.6% in songwriting, and 2.6% in producing. Additionally, on the producing front, the small percentage it holds dropped from 5% with already any women of colour as a producer being in a 180:1 ratio in comparison to white male producers. However, one positive is from the Annenberg Inclusion Initiative reporting that people of colour in both genders rose from 31.2% in 2013, to 59% in 2020.

Unfortunately, changes in the system of the music industry are not going to happen overnight. All that we can really hope for is for women to keep pursuing their dreams in the entertainment business, and women, but more so men, give them the opportunity to put their creativity into action and acknowledge their work when they make something incredible. Only then will the divide in gender become equal, and there will be no repeats in the struggles of women becoming legendary singer-songwriting divas.

References

Addley, E. (2008, June 9). Crime: Amy Winehouse's husband pleads guilty to GBH and cover-up. The Guardian. https://www.theguardian.com/uk/2008/jun/10/ukcrime.amywinehouse

Amy Winehouse. (n.d.). GRAMMY.com. Retrieved September 9, 2021, from https://www.grammy.com/grammys/artists/amy-winehouse/15694

Amy Winehouse, Blake Fielder-Civil granted divorce. (2009, July 16). Billboard. https://www.billboard.com/articles/news/268050/amy-winehouse-blake-fielder-civil-granted-divorce/

Aretha Franklin performs at Kennedy Centre Honors celebrating Carole King. (n.d.). www.caroleking.com. Retrieved September 13, 2021, from https://www.caroleking.com/gallery/video/aretha-franklin-performs-kennedy-center-honors-celebrating-carole-king

Aswad, J. (2021, June 15). The music industry has a long way to go on diversity, USC Annenberg report concludes. Variety. https://variety.com/2021/music/news/music-industry-diversity-usc-annenberg-report-1234996163/

Backwoods glam. (2006, November 30). The Washington Times. https://www.washingtontimes.com/news/2006/nov/30/20061130-090454-4103r/

Beaumont-Thomas, B. (2020, March 6). Number of female UK songwriters jumps by 60%. The Guardian. https://www.theguardian.com/music/2020/mar/06/number-of-female-uk-songwriters-jumps-by-60

Behind the Music: Cher (1999) (full documentary). (2018, June 7). Www.youtube.com. https://www.youtube.com/watch?v=VGWrxldROLw&ab_channel=CherNews

Bertram, C. (2020, January 28). Fleetwood Mac: Behind the drama, divorce and drugs that fuelled the making of "Rumours." Biography. https://www.biography.com/news/fleetwood-mac-rumours-album

Beyoncé talks about her athleisure brand Ivy Park and the pressure to be perfect. (2015, November 26). The Telegraph. https://www.telegraph.co.uk/fashion/brands/beyonce-topshop-athleisure-brand-everything-we-know-information/?utm_source=pocket_mylist

Bio | Carole King. (n.d.). Caroleking.com. Retrieved September 14, 2021, from https://caroleking.com/bio

Bobby Bones Show. (2017, October 9). Dolly Parton interview with Bobby Bones. Www.youtube.com. https://www.youtube.com/watch?v=z48gLpOn_SA&ab_channel=BobbyBonesShow

Bonin, L. (2003, October 23). Cher's tour is the most successful ever by a woman. EW.com. https://ew.com/article/2003/10/31/chers-tour-most-successful-ever-woman/

Bouwman, K. (2004, February 23). "interview with Darcus Beese, A&R at Island for Amy Winehouse, Sugababes. www.hitquarters.com.

http://www.hitquarters.com/index.php3?page=intrvi ew%2Fopar%2Fintrview_Darcus_Beese_int.html

Brown, H. (2016, March 7). Carole King interview: "I didn't have the courage to write songs initially." The   Telegraph. http://www.telegraph.co.uk/journalists/helen-brown/5201808/Carole-King-interview.html

Buskin, R. (2005, September). CLASSIC TRACKS: The Pretenders "Back On The Chain Gang." Www.soundonsound.com. https://www.soundonsound.com/people/classic-tracks-pretenders-back-chain-gang

Buskin, R., & Heatley, M. (2010). The definitive illustrated encyclopedia of rock (pp. 148, 278–279). Flame Tree Publishing.

Carole King. (n.d.). Academy of Achievement. Retrieved September 14, 2021, from https://achievement.org/achiever/carole-king/#biography

CHER ~ Jane Pauley Interview pt 1.wmv. (2011, February 23). www.youtube.com. https://www.youtube.com/watch?v=tFrrxIkrPtg&ab _channel=DarkLadyUK

Childers, C. (2015, August 15). When Fleetwood Mac reunited for "The Dance." Ultimate Classic Rock. https://ultimateclassicrock.com/fleetwood-macs-reunion-album-the-dance-turns-15/

Chrissie Hynde. (2016). Reckless : my life as a pretender (pp. 1–41). Anchor Books.

Chrissie   Hynde.   (2016,   September   6). www.cbsnews.com. https://www.cbsnews.com/pictures/chrissie-hynde/

Chrissie Hynde and The Pretenders. (2009, April 7). PETA.   https://www.peta.org/features/chrissie-hynde-pretenders/

Coleman, A. (2008, December 7). Amy Winehouse Birmingham show ends in chaos. IcBirmingham. http://icbirmingham.icnetwork.co.uk/wow/music/arc hive/tm_method%3Dfull%26objectid%3D2011083 0%26siteid%3D50002-name_page.html

Complete National Recording Registry listing. (2015). The Library of Congress. https://www.loc.gov/programs/national-recording-preservation-board/recording-registry/complete-national-recording-registry-listing/

Cragg, M. (2013, July 5). Björk's Debut: celebrating 20 years of innovation. The Guardian. https://www.theguardian.com/music/musicblog/20 13/jul/05/bjork-debut-20-years-of-innovation

Davies, C. (2011, October 26). Amy Winehouse inquest records verdict of misadventure. The Guardian. https://www.theguardian.com/music/2011/oct/26/a my-winehouse-verdict-misadventure

Davis, S. (2018). Gold Dust Woman : The biography of Stevie Nicks. Centre Point Large Print.

Day, E. (2013, June 22). Growing up with my sister Amy Winehouse. The Guardian. https://www.theguardian.com/music/2013/jun/23/a my-winehouse-growing-up-sister

Deriso, N. (2015, April 14). Fleetwood Mac hit big with "Tango in the Night," then imploded. Something Else! http://somethingelsereviews.com/2015/04/14/fleet wood-mac-tango-in-the-night/

Diane Warren | Songwriters Hall of Fame. (n.d.). Www.songhall.org. Retrieved September 6, 2021, from https://www.songhall.org/profile/Diane_Warren

Drew, I. (2020, May 4). How Cher is combatting Coronavirus. Billboard.

https://www.billboard.com/articles/news/9370577/c
her-coronavirus-interview

Duke, A. (2009, January 12). Amy Winehouse's
husband seeks divorce. CNN.
http://www.cnn.com/2009/SHOWBIZ/Music/01/12/
winehouse.divorce/index.html

Eliscu, J. (2007, June 14). Amy Winehouse: The diva
and her demons. Rolling Stone.
https://www.rollingstone.com/music/music-
news/amy-winehouse-the-diva-and-her-demons-
189641/

Everley, D. (2017, October 2). Mick Fleetwood:
"Fleetwood Mac is the most abused franchise in
the business." Classic Rock Magazine; Louder.
https://www.loudersound.com/features/mick-
fleetwood-fleetwood-mac-is-the-most-abused-
franchise-in-the-business

First Grand Ole Opry performance. (1959, July 25).
Dolly Parton. https://dollyparton.com/life-and-
career/awards_milestones/grand-ole-opry-
performance-1959

Flippo, C. (1980, December 11). The unsinkable Dolly
Parton. Rolling Stone.
https://www.rollingstone.com/music/music-
country/the-unsinkable-dolly-parton-197779/

Forrest, E. (2021, April 30). Leaders in the mix:
Pioneering female music producers to know.
UDiscover Music.
https://www.udiscovermusic.com/stories/pioneerin
g-female-music-producers/

Frank, A. (2016, January 13). Aretha Franklin on the
"Natural Woman" performance that made
President Obama cry. Vogue.
https://www.vogue.com/article/aretha-franklin-
interview-carole-king

Fricke, D. (1988, July 14). The Sugarcubes: The coolest band in the world. Rolling Stone. https://www.rollingstone.com/music/music-news/the-sugarcubes-the-coolest-band-in-the-world-75327/

Green, M. (1991, August 5). Sonny on Cher. People.com. https://people.com/archive/sonny-on-cher-vol-36-no-4/

Grow, K. (2020, July 17). The unsinkable Chrissie Hynde. Rolling Stone. https://www.rollingstone.com/music/music-features/chrissie-hynde-pretenders-new-album-1029689/

Haack, B. (2018, January 19). What happened? 50th Grammy flashback. GRAMMY.com. https://www.grammy.com/grammys/news/alicia-keys-amy-winehouse-7-happenings-50th-grammy-awards

Halperin, S. (2019, February 5). Women in music? The song remains the same, Annenberg study shows. Variety. https://variety.com/2019/music/news/women-in-music-annenberg-inclusion-study-report-1203128562/

Hattenstone, S. (2020, December 14). Cher at 74: "There are 20-year-old girls who can't do what I do." The Guardian. https://www.theguardian.com/culture/2020/dec/14/cher-at-74-there-are-20-year-old-girls-who-cant-do-what-i-do

Hello, I'm Dolly. (1967, February 13). Dolly Parton. https://dollyparton.com/life-and-career/music/hello-im-dolly-album

Holden, S. (1992, April 20). Madonna Makes a $60 Million Deal. The New York Times. https://www.nytimes.com/1992/04/20/arts/madonn

a-makes-a-60-million-
deal.html?utm_source=pocket_mylist

Home. (n.d.). Amy Winehouse Foundation. Retrieved September 12, 2021, from https://amywinehousefoundation.org/

Hopper, J. (2015, January 21). The invisible woman: A conversation with Björk. Pitchfork. https://pitchfork.com/features/interview/9582-the-invisible-woman-a-conversation-with-bjork/

Howard, J. (2013). Cher : strong enough. Plexus.

Jackson, L. M. (2020, October 8). The United States of Dolly Parton. The New Yorker. https://www.newyorker.com/magazine/2020/10/19/the-united-states-of-dolly-parton?utm_source=pocket_mylist

Kalnitz, M. (2021, January 19). Dolly Parton turns 75 today — here's how she went from a poor childhood in rural Tennessee to become one of the most beloved performers of all time. Insider. https://www.insider.com/dolly-parton-life-career-timeline-2020-12

King, C. (2012). A natural woman : a memoir. Grand Central.

Lee, M. (2020, April 1). Dolly Parton announces $1 million donation to Vanderbilt for COVID-19 research. WJHL. https://www.wjhl.com/local-coronavirus-coverage/dolly-parton-announces-she-will-donate-1-million-to-vanderbilt-for-covid-19-research/

Leech, J. (2021, July 27). Why Bobbie Gentry is so much more than "Ode to Billie Joe." UDiscover Music. https://www.udiscovermusic.com/stories/bobbie-gentry-pioneering-female-musician/

Locker, M. (2016, November 9). Chrissie Hynde: "I am very grateful to punk." The Guardian.

https://www.theguardian.com/music/2016/nov/09/c
hrissie-hynde-interview-pretenders

Madonna - Like A Virgin (live MTV VMAs 1984). (2018). In www.youtube.com. https://www.youtube.com/watch?v=gkSxhG4cbPo &ab_channel=Madonna

Madonna, Britney Spears, Christina Aguilera & Missy Eliot - Like A Virgin/Hollywood (VMA 2003) 4K. (2019). In www.youtube.com. https://www.youtube.com/watch?v=xJQM89lmngc &ab_channel=RECuervoAV

Material Girl. (n.d.). Iconix. Retrieved September 20, 2021, from https://www.iconixbrand.com/brands/material-girl/

McFadden, C. (2001, September 7). Stevie Nicks in her own words. ABC News. https://abcnews.go.com/2020/story?id=132659&pa ge=1

Michaels, S. (2010, July 16). Amy Winehouse promises new album for January 2011. The Guardian. https://www.theguardian.com/music/2010/jul/16/a my-winehouse-new-album-2011

Middle 8. (2020, May 29). How Beyoncé made Lemonade. www.youtube.com. https://www.youtube.com/watch?v=f5SxGTe_t4I& ab_channel=Middle8

Milano, B. (2021, March 29). Best female songwriters: An essential top 25 countdown. UDiscover Music. https://www.udiscovermusic.com/stories/best-female-songwriters/

Mizoguchi, K. (2015, December 12). Lady Gaga calls music industry a "f---king boys club." People.com. https://people.com/celebrity/lady-gaga-calls-music-industry-a-f-king-boys-club/

Mulholland, G. (2004, February 1). Charmed and dangerous. The Guardian. https://www.theguardian.com/music/2004/feb/01/p opandrock.amywinehouse

Mullen, M. (2019, June 11). Madonna's now-famous "Like a Virgin" performance was thanks to a wardrobe malfunction. Biography. https://www.biography.com/news/madonna-like-a-virgin-vmas-1984

Nissim, M. (2009, September 8). Young: "We never expelled Winehouse." Digital Spy. https://www.digitalspy.com/showbiz/a176379/youn g-we-never-expelled-winehouse/

Nissim, M. (2012, July 13). Mitch Winehouse playlist tribute to Amy. Digital Spy. https://www.digitalspy.com/music/a393206/amy-winehouse-music-playlist-mitch-chooses-the-songs-of-amys-life/

Parton, D., & Schmidt, R. (2017). Dolly on Dolly : interview and encounters. Chicago Review Press.

Paulson, D. (2015, December 26). Dolly Parton remembers writing "I Will Always Love You." The Tennessean. https://www.tennessean.com/story/entertainment/ music/2015/12/26/dolly-parton-remembers-writing-always-love-you/77762172/

Perone, J. E. (2007). The words and music of Carole King (pp. 2–26). Praeger ; Northam.

Price, S. (2014, June 10). Talker of the town: Chrissie Hynde interviewed by simon price. The Quietus. https://thequietus.com/articles/15484-chrissie-hynde-interview-simon-price

Punk rock: 30 years of subversion. (2006, August 18). News.bbc.co.uk. http://news.bbc.co.uk/2/hi/entertainment/5263364. stm

Pytilk, M. (2007, May 8). Björk: Volta. Pitchfork. https://pitchfork.com/reviews/albums/10204-volta/
Pytilk, M. (2011, October 13). Björk: Biophilia. Pitchfork. https://pitchfork.com/reviews/albums/15915-biophilia/
Pytlik, M. (2003). Björk : wow and flutter. Aurum.
Raising Malawi. (n.d.). Raising Malawi. Retrieved September 22, 2021, from https://www.raisingmalawi.org/
Reubin, R. A., & G. Beil, R. (1911, March 25). Women composers in American popular song, page 1. Parlorsongs.com. http://parlorsongs.com/issues/2002-9/thismonth/feature.php
Rice, L. (7201, July 23). Amy Winehouse: CBS exec remembers singer's 2008 Grammy performance. EW.com. https://ew.com/article/2011/07/23/amy-winehouse-dead-grammy-remember/
Riley, D. (2018, August 16). Stating the obvious, Amy Winehouse fears early death. The Inquisitr. https://www.inquisitr.com/13488/stating-the-obvious-amy-winehouse-fears-early-death/
Robertson, E. (n.d.). Björk. The Talks. Retrieved September 22, 2021, from https://the-talks.com/interview/bjork/?utm_source=pocket_my list
Rosenthal, N. (2020, July 1). The truth about Don Henley and Stevie Nicks' relationship. Grunge.com. https://www.grunge.com/223092/the-truth-about-don-henley-and-stevie-nicks-relationship/
Sandall, R. (2008, October 7). Can Amy Winehouse be saved? Times Online. http://entertainment.timesonline.co.uk/tol/arts_and_entertainment/music/article4383952.ece

Sawyer, M. (2017, November 12). Björk: "People miss the jokes. A lot of it is me taking the piss out of myself." The Guardian. https://www.theguardian.com/music/2017/nov/12/bjork-utopia-interview-people-miss-the-jokes

Schreiber, R. (2001, July 31). Björk: Vespertine. Pitchfork. https://pitchfork.com/reviews/albums/727-vespertine/

Schwartz, M. (2003, September 23). Why Madonna's new book is worth checking out. EW.com. https://ew.com/article/2003/09/26/why-madonnas-new-book-worth-checking-out/

Sessums, K. (1990, November 1). Cher: Star-Studded. Vanity Fair. https://www.vanityfair.com/news/1990/11/cher-199011?utm_source=pocket_mylist

Shakerley, T. (2020, May 20). 5 female producers proving it's A woman's game too. Cool Accidents Music Blog. https://www.coolaccidents.com/news/women-producers-changing-the-game

Shaw, L. (2021, March 8). Female artists struggle to make gains in pop music, study finds - BNN Bloomberg. BNN Bloomberg. https://www.bnnbloomberg.ca/female-artists-struggle-to-make-gains-in-pop-music-study-finds-1.1573910

Sheffield, R. (2017, February 3). Rob Sheffield on why Fleetwood Mac's "Rumours" hits home right now. Rolling Stone. https://www.rollingstone.com/music/music-features/why-fleetwood-macs-rumours-hits-home-right-now-121403/

Siffrinn, B., & Skidmore-William, A. (2021, June 22). The Making of Madonna | B*tch I'm Madonna (No. 4). Wondery.

Siffrinn, B., & Skidmore-Williams, A. (2021a, April 27). Beyonce and Jay-Z | Crazy in Love (No. 1). Wondery.

Siffrinn, B., & Skidmore-Williams, A. (2021b, May 4). Beyonce and Jay-Z | Run the World (No. 2). Wondery.

Siffrinn, B., & Skidmore-Williams, A. (2021c, May 11). Beyonce and Jay-Z | Love on Top (No. 3). Wondery.

Siffrinn, B., & Skidmore-Williams, A. (2021d, May 18). Beyonce and Jay-Z | Lemonade (No. 4). Wondery.

Siffrinn, B., & Skidmore-Williams, A. (2021e, June 1). The Making of Madonna | Blonde Ambition (No. 1). Wondery.

Siffrinn, B., & Skidmore-Williams, A. (2021f, June 8). The Making of Madonna | Who's That Girl (No. 2). Wondery.

Siffrinn, B., & Skidmore-Williams, A. (2021g, June 15). The Making of Madonna | Borderline (No. 3). Wondery.

Sisario, B. (2018, January 25). Gender diversity in the music industry? The numbers are grim. The New York Times. https://www.nytimes.com/2018/01/25/arts/music/music-industry-gender-study-women-artists-producers.html

Smith, Dr. S. L., Pieper, Dr. K., Clark, H., Case, A., & Choueiti, M. (2020). Inclusion in the recording studio? Gender and race/ethnicity of artists, songwriters & producers across 800 popular songs from 2012-2019. In Annenberg Inclusion Initiative (pp. 2–6). Annenberg Inclusion Initiative.

https://assets.uscannenberg.org/docs/aii-inclusion-recording-studio-20200117.pdf

Strauss, N. (1999, March 11). Cher resurrected, again, by a hit; the long, hard but serendipitous road to "Believe." The New York Times. https://www.nytimes.com/1999/03/11/arts/cher-resurrected-again-by-a-hit-the-long-hard-but-serendipitous-road-to-believe.html?utm_source=pocket_mylist

Sturges, F. (2011, October 23). Amy Winehouse: singer who won the hearts of millions but was unable to overcome her dependency on drink and drugs. The Independent. https://www.independent.co.uk/news/obituaries/amy-winehouse-singer-who-won-hearts-millions-was-unable-overcome-her-dependency-drink-and-drugs-2319847.html

Talevski, N. (2006). Knocking on heaven's door : rock obituaries. Omnibus.

Tannenbaum, R. (2014, September 26). Stevie Nicks admits past pregnancy with Don Henley and more about her wild history. Billboard. https://www.billboard.com/articles/news/6266329/stevie-nicks-interview-on-don-henley-fleetwood-mac-24-karat-gold-album

The John F. Kennedy Center for the Performing Arts - our story. (n.d.). Www.kennedy-Center.org. Retrieved September 13, 2021, from https://www.kennedy-center.org/our-story/

The Porter Wagoner Show welcomes Dolly Parton. (1967, August 13). Dolly Parton. https://dollyparton.com/life-and-career/movies-television/the-porter-wagoner-show/660

Udovich, M. (1994, November 17). Bjork: The world's only cheerful Icelandic surrealist. Rolling Stone. https://www.rollingstone.com/music/music-news/bjork-the-worlds-only-cheerful-icelandic-surrealist-196284/

Valenti, L. (2019, November 21). Dolly Parton reveals she recorded "9 to 5" using her acrylic nails as an instrument. Vogue. https://www.vogue.com/article/dolly-parton-long-acrylic-nails-instrument-9-to-5

Wang, A. X. (2021, March 8). Women in music dwindled in 2020. Rolling Stone. https://www.rollingstone.com/pro/news/women-artists-music-study-2021-1138094/

WatchMojo. (2011, September 28). The life and career of Bjork. www.youtube.com. https://www.youtube.com/watch?v=hNQDYBKj7FQ&ab_channel=WatchMojo.com

Whaley, N. (2018, November 15). Beyoncé buys Ivy Park stake from Topshop owner accused of sexual harassment and racial abuse. Mic. https://www.mic.com/articles/192482/beyonce-buys-ivy-park-stake-from-topshop-owner-accused-of-sexual-harassment-and-racial-abuse

Who is Carole King? Everything You Need to Know. (n.d.). Www.thefamouspeople.com. Retrieved September 14, 2021, from https://www.thefamouspeople.com/profiles/carole-king-8941.php

Who is Chrissie Hynde? Everything you need to know. (n.d.). Www.thefamouspeople.com. Retrieved September 16, 2021, from https://www.thefamouspeople.com/profiles/chrissie-hynde-40935.php

Whyte, B. (2019, September 11). Black women in pop music are still held to an impossible standard. Bitch Media. https://www.bitchmedia.org/article/normani-critiques-history-of-black-women-pop-artists

Williams, M. (2014, May 28). Chrissie Hynde: "Malcolm McLaren wanted me to dress up like a guy." The Guardian. https://www.theguardian.com/music/2014/may/28/chrissie-hynde-interview-the-pretenders-malcolm-mclaren

Williamson, N. (2013, January 29). Fleetwood Mac: "Everybody was pretty weirded out" – the story of Rumours. UNCUT. https://www.uncut.co.uk/features/fleetwood-mac-everybody-was-pretty-weirded-out-the-story-of-rumours-26395/

Yandoli, K. L. (2016, November 24). The full story behind how the "Gilmore Girls" theme song came to be. BuzzFeed. https://www.buzzfeed.com/krystieyandoli/where-you-lead-i-will-follow

Yglesias, A. M. (2021, July 23). Watch Amy Winehouse win ROTY for "Rehab" in 2008. GRAMMY.com. https://www.grammy.com/grammys/news/amy-winehouse-wins-record-year-rehab-2008-grammy-rewind

Zehme, B. (1989, March 23). Madonna: The Rolling Stone Interview. Rolling Stone. https://www.rollingstone.com/music/music-news/madonna-the-rolling-stone-interview-103058/

Zoladz, L. (2017, November 21). The enduring power of Stevie Nicks. The Ringer. https://www.theringer.com/music/2017/11/21/16683772/stevie-nicks-book-career-fleetwood-mac

Printed in Great Britain
by Amazon

17288366R00078